REINVENTED LIVES

REINVENTED LIVES

Women at Sixty: A Celebration

Elizabeth & Charles Handy

HUTCHINSON
LONDON

Published in 2002 by Hutchinson

3 5 7 9 10 8 6 4 2

Hutchinson
The Random House Group Limited
20 Vauxhall Bridge Road, London SW1V 2SA

Random House Australia (Pty) Limited
20 Alfred Street, Milsons Point, Sydney
New South Wales 2061, Australia

Random House New Zealand Limited
18 Poland Road, Glenfield,
Auckland 10, New Zealand

Random House (Pty) Limited
Endulini, 5a Jubilee Road, Parktown 2193,
South Africa

The Random House Group Limited Reg. No. 954009
www.randomhouse.co.uk

A CIP catalogue record for this book is available
from the British Library

ISBN 9780091793586

The Random House Group Limited supports the Forest Stewardship
Council® (FSC®), the leading international forest-certification organisation.
Our books carrying the FSC label are printed on FSC®-certified paper.
FSC is the only forest-certification scheme supported by the leading environmental
organisations, including Greenpeace. Our paper procurement policy can be found at
www.randomhouse.co.uk/environment

Design/make up by Roger Walker

Printed and bound in Great Britain by
MPG Printgroup

The book is dedicated to every woman who is approaching sixty and is perhaps wondering what the rest of life holds in store. We hope that she will gain encoragement and inspiration from the very varied stories recounted here and from the women who have told them.

Contents

Acknowledgements

Our thanks go firstly to the twenty-eight women who allowed us into their lives, who sat for their portraits and then agreed to write their own story of their life. They are the real authors of this book. It is no easy matter to compress the adventures, thoughts and feelings of a lifetime into fifteen hundred words. We were delighted that they accepted the challenge so willingly and delivered so eloquently.

Our editor, Paul Sidey, has given us his constant support and encouragement during the book's long gestation. We are very appreciative of his unfailing belief in us and what we are seeking to do. Backing him up are the team at Hutchinson and Random House. It is only when we, the authors, walk into a meeting with the planning group that we fully realise how many people are involved in making our collection of words and photographs into a pleasing book on your bookshelf. We are grateful to them all for their interest in this project and for the help that they have given us.

Elizabeth and Charles Handy

Diss, Norfolk, England

CHARLES HANDY

Introduction

I t was at the sixtieth birthday party of a friend that it struck us: sixty is no longer what it used to be – not for women, anyway. Our hostess, the focus of the celebrations, set the mood of the group when she spoke of her hopes for the next decade, when she would be free to do more of the things she had postponed for so long while she had done a series of jobs and high-profile public roles as well as raising a family and caring for ageing parents. We had, it should be admitted, a personal interest. Elizabeth was about to be sixty herself, an event she looked forward to with a mixture of apprehension and excitement. What, we both wondered, would her sixties hold? She had only recently been able to give more time to her passion and profession – portrait photography.

11

Would her art flower in her sixties or was her best soon to be behind her?

Our hostess had given us immediate reassurance. She and the friends she had gathered around her that day made age seem irrelevant, a thing of the mind not the body. 'So this is what sixty is like these days,' we thought as we looked around the room. It wasn't just the looks. Where our mothers had been tired, even worn-out, by this age, and where many of the husbands present were even now talking of retirement, the women that afternoon were often at the peak of their lives and had no intention of stopping. They might have been born sixty or more years ago but they clearly felt about forty in their heads. Many of them were actively reinventing themselves, planning to start something new, to live in a different way or in a different place, perhaps with a different companion. They spoke of choices, of lives freed up. The future beckoned.

We realised then that we were looking at individuals from an unusual generation, one that would come to be seen as a new chapter in our social history. For the first time, most women born sixty years ago now have the chance of an extra chunk of healthy life, at least ten years more than previous generations enjoyed. On average, says the government actuary, a sixty-year-old woman can today expect to live for another twenty-two years. And since that is an average figure, a half or thereabouts will live even longer. A century ago the average woman would not even make sixty – the expectation of life at birth was forty-nine. Of course, there have always been older women living interesting lives well into their eighties, but they were the exception. Now they could become the norm. That's new and that should be news because here is a whole cohort of women who have been handed an extra slice of life that they could not have counted on, could not reasonably have expected when they were young and probably never planned for.

Because life is known to be longer now, many feel that they can postpone some of life's stages. Even ageing, it seems, can now be put on hold. Ironically, however, these bonus years may not be the pattern for women in subsequent generations. Many of the next generation are marrying later. They are starting careers and postponing their families and should, therefore, be free of them later, too. They are using up the extra ten years in their youth. The women we were talking to are getting the benefit of a longer life in its latter half. Most of them were already multiple grandmothers, their own children independent and their parents, in most cases, departed. When today's young reach sixty in their turn they may well find that both children and parents are still dependent on them. They won't be free, as most of these women were, to shape fresh futures for themselves. In that sense, this generation of sixty-year-olds may turn out to be unique.

Governments worry, a little belatedly, about these longer lives. Who, in particular, is going to pay for what officials, rather disparagingly, call the new elderly? But the women we were talking to were not old, even though they rejoiced in their free bus passes and concessionary tickets. Governments inevitably calculate the downsides, but we, that day, pondered the full range of possibilities that might be released by this gift of extra life. We decided, as we returned from the party, that we would seek out a selection of other women now in their sixties. If this extended life is going to be the norm for a while, society will need new models for a life past sixty.

We set out to find a range of different people, some whom we knew, most of whom we did not: between twenty-five and thirty individuals all told, we thought, enough to provide a variety of experiences and backgrounds, but not so many that the individual stories would get swamped. Elizabeth would photograph them, because we wanted to show what sixty looks like today, and we would ask them to write their own scripts – what it felt like to be in their sixties, what they were doing now and how they got there. That way we would not run the risk of unintentionally imposing our own interpretations on their lives. My own role, as a writer, would be limited to editing their scripts and writing this introduction. The result would be a collection of individual women at sixty speaking, or rather writing, for themselves.

This book is the result.

It is not a sociological study. There are no big numbers here that could be used to justify any grand conclusions. That was not our aim. Instead, we have gathered together twenty-eight examples of women in their sixties, portraits of individuals in words and pictures. It is our hope that every woman reading the book should be able to identify with at least one story, because the book is, in effect, a collection of short stories about the lives of ordinary women who, when you investigate, aren't ordinary at all, who have lived and are living interesting and sometimes extraordinary lives. Looking at the portraits first, it is striking how different they are. There is no one image of a woman at sixty. The stories that they have written underline the different paths they have taken and their varied designs for their futures. There are no rules.

Some have arrived at sixty after experiencing the emptiness that follows the death of their husband, or after divorce. One woman has remained single from choice all her life. Everyone has been through one or other of the traumas of life, from the death of an only son or a beloved mother, to serious illness, financial hardship, enforced retirement or the challenge of coming out as a lesbian. They are stories to give one hope, because these women have found that the sixties are what Gail Sheehy, the American author of *Passages*, called the Age of Integrity, the time when you are finally and fully yourself. Erik Erikson, the psychoanalyst expert on identity, described it this way: 'A state of mind assured of order and meaning with the serenity to bless and defend one's own life history.' The stories here put flesh on the bare bones of this definition.

There are people here who are well-known, such as Anita Roddick and Prue Leith, celebrated now but who started from less glamorous beginnings. There are some who have a higher public profile than others, like Dame Rennie Fritchie, who began life in a council house in Scotland but has entered her sixties as the Commissioner in charge of overseeing all the public appointments in the UK. Others, such as Audrey Eyton of *The F-Plan Diet*, have enjoyed a high profile and success in the past but have now moved on to other interests. Success, anyway, needs to be redefined at this stage in life. No longer is it a matter of fame or fortunes, if it ever was. After sixty, it seems, what the world thinks matters less than what you believe to be the real priorities. All these women, therefore, could be called successful, whether we have heard of them or not, because their lives are as they want them to be.

Perhaps for that reason they would all be classified as middle-class, if that is defined as being in control of one's life and having the means to do so, but not all of the women started out that way. One message comes through clearly – you can be whatever you want to be in your sixties and do whatever you want to do, no matter where you start from. Even in our more open society that message still needs to be heard. At sixty, Kathryn Kirkland-Handley decided to give up her home and counselling work in Richmond, London and become a potter in America, splitting her life between her studio in the New Mexico desert and living with her new husband for part of the year back in London. Meredith Hooper fulfilled a lifetime's dream and went off to Antarctica as official writer in residence at a research station, leaving her family to cope without her for four months at a time. Carole Stone married for the first time in her late fifties and embarked on her career as networker extraordinary, with 16,000 names on file and her salons crowded with the great and the good. There are more such stories. But part of the fascination lies in their accounts of how they got there and where they started from.

The group is diverse in its origins. They all now live for at least part of the year in Britain or Ireland, but some came originally from America or from the Caribbean or India, as well as from South Africa, England, Ireland and Scotland. Allegra Taylor had a Polish father and grew up variously in California, Brazil and Canada. More exotically still, Levana Marshall boasts a family from Greece of Spanish-Israeli descent, and is married to an Indian Jew. The women are all different, not only in their origins, but in their occupations and their perspectives. Levana Marshall herself is a psychotherapist with, as you might expect, the best perspective on life and living as one gets older. Diana Sharpe is an international lawyer, but she started as a nurse long years before. Winnie Smikle, too, was a nurse, and loved it. When she was declared redundant in her fifties the bottom fell out of her world. Nothing daunted, she opened a small nursing home of her own in her sixties.

Others, like Brenda Weir, married young and devoted many years to building and managing a family, waiting until her sixties to feel free to be fully herself. Wendy Ball was mother to six, wife to one and conference organiser to thousands. She is now, among other things, a prize-winning garden designer. Camilla Panufnik is a writer and photographer but her husband, a distinguished composer, and their children, filled her life until he died. Patricia Moberly was a teacher all her life until, in her sixties, she became the chairman of a great London hospital. Shirley Daniels was a teacher and then head teacher, until she resigned in protest because the Education Authority took away her sixth form. Now, in her sixties, she runs her dream school – in the United Arab Emirates. Claire Evans, like many others, started life as a secretary, married and ended up as a diplomat's wife. When he retired she concentrated on her love of music, producing operas with friends in small theatres in England and Italy. Gillian Reckitt also started as a secretary and after an adventurous life now runs a café in Whitstable with her daughter as chef. Prue Leith, on the other hand, gave up her restaurant and cookery school before she was sixty and branched out, writing best-selling novels among many other things.

Rosemary Hamilton, however, has been an interior designer all her life, never marrying, never wanting to. Pauline Bewick, too, has never wavered from her early passion for art and is now in full flower as one of Ireland's most successful artists. Allegra Taylor has always been a writer although her topics range widely, and Levana Marshall has always been a psychologist and psychotherapist. Some don't change at sixty, they just blossom. Others blossom in a new marriage, like Rosemary Hopkins and Catherine Warner. Jane Freebairn-Smith blossomed when, nearly sixty, she was ordained a priest and now has her own parish in Lincolnshire.

All of them different in different ways.

Being a woman at sixty is becoming fashionable, but it is not yet everywhere understood or appreciated. There are the iconic media personalities such as Joan Collins and Tina Turner who seem to defy their years, yet to some their lives seem almost indecent. 'Why can't they act their age?' ask their disapproving, or maybe envious, contemporaries. Nearer home, public personalities such as Joan Bakewell, Sue MacGregor, Margaret Jay and others have entered their sixties with their energies and their love of life as fierce as ever. It is, unfortunately, too easy to dismiss these as exceptions. Society's stereotypes linger long. It was Joan Bakewell who described a visit to a children's ward in a hospital where she met a little girl who showed her the dolls she was playing with. 'There was this doll with crinkly grey hair and little spectacles on the end of her nose and wearing slippers with bobs on. "What's that?" I asked, and she said, "That's granny." "But I'm a granny," I said. "Look at me, this is what grannies look like. We wear high heels, nice clothes and have lives. I'm a granny and I work and I go to the gym and I've just bought myself a sporty little car.'" More examples like Joan Bakewell are needed if we are to persuade everyone, including the doll makers, that the world has changed. We hope that the women in this book will add the weight of their testimonies so that more people will be able to act their age in a similar way.

The testimonies lead you through their very different lives. These are potted autobiographies, privileged glimpses of personal lives, loves and careers. Looking back from where they stand now, there is a discernible pattern in each of their stories, even if that pattern emerged unplanned and was unintended at the beginning. You can often see continuity only in retrospect. Allegra Taylor describes it as 'life's tapestry'. Anita Roddick sees the past as the prologue to a new future, a play, perhaps, with several acts still to come, while Jane Freebairn-Smith sees a golden thread running through her life, drawing her on. The point is that one cannot look at one's sixties in isolation. They are inevitably shaped by what went before. We should never dismiss the past; it is the basis for our futures.

The twenty-eight life tapestries may all be different but there are some common threads.

1   The first thing that strikes the reader is how different the lives of these women have been from those of the men of their time – and probably from the lives that their daughters or granddaughters will lead. Life for the women in the book seems to have been a collage of different tasks and commitments. It is a collage that was and is constantly changing as commitments change, flexilife writ large. For many of them the collage was constructed around the career of the husband. As the biblical Ruth says, 'Where you go I will go, where you lodge I will lodge, your people will be my people and your God my God.' Ruth was talking to her mother-in-law after the death of her husband, because it was the same

contract that she had made with her husband. That contract hadn't changed over the millennia for most women until the advent of the dual-career family in more recent times. Most of the women in this book speak of fitting their own work into the cracks in their other commitments. Meredith Hooper explains how it was for most: 'It was the way we were brought up. The assumptions welded deep in our beings. Girls were, as they always had been, for marrying, ideally by twenty-one, certainly not too much later. When I fell in love I wrote in my diary, with not a hint of irony, or question, "Farewell career."'

2   Meredith Hooper is unusual in this collection because she went to university. Most of them did not. As Joanna Foster says, 'I was the product of a girls' boarding school, two brothers and the parental expectation that they would go to university and I would do a secretarial course.' In Rennie Fritchie's case she left school early in order to work in her father's hotel: 'The hotel was the reason that I left school before my sixteenth birthday. It seemed much more exciting to work in the hotel than continue to study and, in any case, in those days higher education was not something thought of as desirable for girls in our family.' University, if it came at all, had to be experienced later, as Allegra Taylor did: 'While our children were young I attempted to fill in some of the lamentable gaps in my own schooling and eventually achieved a London University B.Ed. degree with music as a special subject.' Only if teaching was your chosen career, as it was for Shirley Daniels, did most women think of going to university. They were not atypical of their time. Less than ten per cent of the young in Britain then went on to higher education and the great majority of those were male.

As a result most women who wanted to work had only the choice of factory or shop jobs or, if they hankered after something different, nursing or secretarial work. For many, therefore, an early marriage and children offered a preferable life. Today over thirty per cent of young people go on to higher or further education and seventy per cent are still studying at eighteen, a figure that the government hopes will rise to nearer a hundred. The result is a much wider range of opportunities for everyone, but particularly for women. This, combined with the pill and new social norms, has changed the lives of women in ways that would have been unimaginable when the women in our sample were young. In the words of Betty Friedan women have begun to 'take over the day', competing with men in the workplace, with careers jostling for priority with marriage and childbearing. The ripple effects of these changes will mean that to be a woman at sixty will be different once again from the experience of their predecessors.

3   It is noticeable that in only two of the stories is the word 'retirement' mentioned. Maybe it is a gender tradition, in the sense that women's work is never done, whether it be mothering, house management, or what Camilla Panufnik calls 'wifing', with no retirement possible until and unless they all die or depart. Retirement is not a word that women tend to use, except in a narrow technical sense. Diana Sharpe does record that at sixty she was forcibly retired (note the transitive verb – something done to one) because, she was told, it was a young man's world; whereupon she immediately started her own international legal practice. Instead of life being a career with a defined end, all these women have experienced it as a series of episodes. The future is just another episode, different maybe, slower possibly, more self-indulgent perhaps, but not retirement. Pippa Weir has built her life with her second husband around an exotic series of these episodes that have changed every few years, ranging from sailing their own char-

ter yacht in Turkey to, at sixty, setting up a cheese stall in local markets in East Anglia, with more joint enterprises to come, she says. Those who have stuck to one strand of work throughout their lives because they love it see no point in giving it up and, being self-employed, there is no one to 'retire them' forcibly.

It is a cast of mind that everyone will need to adopt in the future, men as well as women. The money that has been promised or accumulated to pay for our later years in the form of pensions was never intended to cover the extra years that most people will now have between leaving full-time work and dying. We depart earlier and die later leaving that extra ten years or so uncovered. 'Retirement' will come to mean 'pensionable' but just as professional swimmers and tennis players, who are entitled by law to draw their pensions in their thirties, would not dream of thinking of themselves as retired, so it will be with us all; 'pensionable' will not mean retired from either work or life. There are messages in the stories of these women that should be heeded by both sexes.

4 We expected that health and physical appearance might be major worries for these women at their age. If so, they treat them lightly. Their portraits surprised some of the women with lines they had forgotten were there, but most took the approach of Anna Magnani who reportedly said to Federico Fellini, 'Don't retouch my wrinkles – it took so long to get them!' The lustre of experience can prove more interesting than the bloom of youth. Nevertheless, Anita Roddick admits, 'I think I'm not quite done yet with the business of being a woman. You know, the whole thing of worrying about what you look like, how you're relating to people, what they're thinking of you.' Then she goes on, 'I hasten to add that I never look at a younger woman and wish I was her. I want to broker time, not looks.'

21

Many mention the irritating physical drawbacks of ageing, those 'senior moments' of forgetfulness, eyes less sharp than they were and aches in new places, but, as Patricia Moberly puts it, when talking of her many illnesses, 'it is of little consequence. The one thing you do not want to do is to clobber everyone else with it and talk about it.'

For some, however, a major illness became a turning point in their lives. Joan Robinson who, on top of a painful divorce and financial worries, had to endure two strokes, a brain operation and a broken jaw, concludes that 'because of what I went through I can now honestly say that I am stronger, more understanding of other people's needs, more positive than I was before, and with a deep spiritual belief that my soul is truly my own. What I need I have, anything I want I can do without.' Reading her story one can only wonder at her resilience and courage.

Brenda Weir, who was gravely ill as she approached sixty, agrees that one can emerge stronger: 'Having the fragility of life brought so close alters one's focus. Essentials are speedily sorted from the inessentials. There is no time and less point in resenting, reproaching and anticipating things "that might happen". Forgiveness of yourself and others is crucial so you can become comfortable with yourself.'

5   A major illness is one of those wake-up calls that make us sit down and take stock of life and what we want from it. The stories resonate with tales of new lives grown out of sadness. Camilla Panufnik whose husband, Andrzej, 'had been the core of my life, my *raison d'être*', was devastated by his death from cancer and found that the first few years passed terrifyingly slowly, with constant reminders rekindling her tears. Eventually, however, life picked up again without leaving the past behind. In addition to being the guardian of her hus-

band's work and memory, she is, she says, 'pulled in all directions by my own professions and by a fascinating but demanding panoply of voluntary work. I still have a huge hole in my life but I'm blessed with a capacity for contentment. I haven't married again. Freedom to abandon home, guiltlessly to go anywhere I want when I want, is a stimulating alternative. I don't think about being sixty years old. I do need sixty hours in every twenty-four.'

Joanna Foster, whose sixtieth birthday party it was that first set us thinking, had a sad epilogue to that happy day. Less than two years later her husband unexpectedly left her for another woman. Like Camilla, she found it hard at first to move on: 'My head has frequently told me that it is time to put all the shocks and horrors behind me and to start rebuilding my life. My heart has lagged painfully behind.' But in time things began to get better. 'It has been a long, staged journey,' she says, 'with many circular diversions and blind alleys. I have learned that living by myself can be enjoyable; that having my children and friends to talk with, play with, eat with and cry with is beyond price; that driving around Europe alone can be fun; that sorting out bills, wilful computers and broken boilers is not; that a good therapist is my lifeline along with e-mail, the telephone and my garden. Embarking on a new life at sixty-two is just beginning to seem exciting.'

For Audrey Eyton the trigger was the death of her only son. 'On Matthew's death I could contemplate no hope of future happiness but simply resolved to be useful, doubly useful for both of us, in the cause we shared. In that resolve I inadvertently found the secret of contentment.' She became an ardent campaigner for animal rights as he had been. She says now, 'The battle to change societies' belief that only man matters is and will now always remain the core of my life.'

In Penelope Lyndon-Stanford's case her mother's death was the catalyst. 'I was devastated. I was very close to my mother. She had been my friend and confidante for most of my grown-up life. After her death I felt that there was nothing left for me to do. It was the end of an era. I was now the older generation and had, I thought, fulfilled all my uses in this world. I had brought up four children and waited until my mother died; it was now time for me to die. I began to think that in the old days, when you had done all this, you probably did die.' Her children were grown, she was single, she decided to take a backpack and travel the world. 'All the young seemed to have had "Gap Years"; why shouldn't I go away and see what would happen? I felt that it had to be some sort of challenge so that I could start living again. I could not just give up.' She came back with her sense of herself restored. 'I think that what nine months travelling by myself has done for me is to make me feel more confident. I now realise that life can be so much fun even as an older woman.'

For Rosemary Hopkins it was the other way round. Instead of losing someone, she met a new man when she had thought that she was going to be single for the rest of her life. 'I had committed myself to making a difference in the world. I was counselling people; I was co-ordinating Traidcraft locally, working to alleviate poverty in the underdeveloped world. Suddenly I was being offered a different path, a chance to love and be loved, to embrace a life of travel and opportunities for further discoveries, and to do all this with a man who shared so many of my passions – nature, the arts, travel, and exploring ways of living more fully and in a relationship.'

It was the same for Catherine Warner. After a long but ultimately unhappy marriage she began to live and love again at sixty. She says, 'How lucky I have been! At my lowest point I met someone who wanted to help, someone who had valued his lost family life and who offered me a strong and steady hand. We have now been married for two years . . . Life is full again, with my new husband. Together we laugh, we talk, we argue, we love our own and each other's families and most of all we love each other. We have to tread carefully with our children. This love thing in the over-sixties is hard for them to understand, while we think our inner sixteen-year-old emotions are well tempered by our ages. My dear friend Rene always said, when her children were being disruptive, "You can't put an old head on young shoulders." I know for certain now that under my old head are some very young shoulders indeed.'

6   It is encouraging to find that life can pick up again, can be fulfilling again, after personal traumas and tragedies. Some have been spared the worst of these, although death and illness are constant companions at this age, of friends and family if not of oneself. Levana Marshall confronts this issue head-on: 'In the last three years I've lost a few of my beloved friends, and my father. I challenge myself to prepare to die . . . I want to be able to smile with compassion to myself on my deathbed (if there's going to be a bed). To smile at the messes I created in my life, for the terrible destructions I was involved in, for the beautiful garden I created, for the deep, deep love I have for Morris, for my children, for life – and for death.'

Not everyone looks on death as a friend and most don't mention it, but every story ends on an upbeat. Perhaps people are reluctant to be pessimistic in print. But maybe we should believe them when they say that life truly can get better. A sense of finally being at ease with oneself, of being comfortable in one's own skin, seems to be the flavour of this age. As Sukey Field puts it, 'For some time now I have been pursuing serenity rather than radical transformation in my life; attempting to get better at doing less, rather than finding new things to do or new ways to be. I want this decade to be one of change and reinvention but not one to be measured by how much I've got done or what radical change I have achieved.'

For Anita Roddick it will, surely, be less quiet than that: 'I believe that a door is opening on a decade when I'll celebrate everything that has come before in my life. I imagine the day must come when I'll look back and see that door closing, and I'm sure that will be a shock. But between then and now, I intend to have fun, *real* fun.' Many would agree with Prue Leith who says that she only does things now that really interest her. It is all right, finally, it seems, to be a little self-indulgent; or just to enjoy Brenda Weir's three Fs of Family, Friends and Fun.

Others might share the more philosophical viewpoint of Allegra Taylor; 'At the age of sixty I ponder the meaning of happiness and wonder if it isn't merely the simple fact of being mindful of each precious day. Futile to mourn the should-have-beens, might-have-beens. Foolish to fear the future. Who knows if there'll be one? Today is all we ever have. Cancer gave me this invaluable perspective – a pleasing sense of the quiet spaciousness of being here now, alongside an acceptance of the immutable law of impermanence.'

There is a general sense in all their testimonies that, at sixty, we can begin to do more things for their own sake rather than for their utility. Our lives become more authentic and maybe that is the best way to prepare for whatever may lie ahead.

7 Somewhat surprisingly, given the difficulties that so many faced in their youth, that ugly word 'feminism' was never mentioned. These women coped with any inequities the world threw at them without needing to take up arms against

them. They just got on with the world as they found it and, where necessary, made it dance to their tune.

With one exception they all got married and several of them repeated the experiment. But, as Anita Roddick points out, marriage at sixty, in this day and age, is different. 'Because men are no longer the centre of women's lives when they reach their sixties. That's truer today than ever before. Women are finding new story-lines . . . They're not preoccupied with the issues that make an ageing man's life such a minefield. They have a new sense of liberation.' In marriage, she says, 'It's the debate, the challenge, the anticipation of things you can do together I've always relished most. In that sense, your relationship with your partner becomes your relationship with the rest of the world.'

If this book proves anything besides the comforting fact that life can be exciting and fulfilling at sixty it is that life is there to be shaped as you want it. In their own stories these women provide vivid evidence of how possible it is, these days, for women to do anything they want to and still remain feminine.

REINVENTED LIVES

ELIZABETH HANDY

The photographer reflects

I never imagined that, at sixty, I would be in the middle of a project like this book or that I would be a portrait photographer when I grew up, but I have never enjoyed my work and my life as much as I do now. At last I am doing something that is really me. It is such a privilege to take someone's portrait. They are allowing you into their lives for a short time and are trusting you with how they look. It is both a challenge and a responsibility because I want them to feel good about it, even, perhaps, to learn something about themselves.

For this book I have entered women's lives at sixty. At other times the portrait might mark an engagement, a wedding or a special anniversary, perhaps the moment when the children finally leave home – personal times. For me portrait photography is a chance to get to know different people from different generations and backgrounds in an intimate way. I love it and I take a secret pleasure when I see my portraits hanging on people's walls or placed in family albums. I like to think that many of my photographs will become part of a family's memory, passed down the generations, that when the digital snaps have long faded my black and white portraits will still be there. Portraits are social history.

My sixtieth birthday present to myself was a new darkroom and workroom. At last I now have my own space and my own mini-gallery. For six weeks I spent every morning in that darkroom processing the photographs for this book, relishing the excitement as I watched the prints emerging in the developing tray. Someone told me that photographers love risk. That must be true, because there are so many things that can go wrong, and there are, anyway, no rules for what a portrait should be. I am always experimenting. For someone who has never liked rules or regulations, photography has proved to be a great outlet for my eccentricity.

I was fifty when I got my degree in photography, but it was not until I was sixty that I started to do work that I felt good about. Unconsciously I waited until the children grew up and most of my elderly relatives had died before I could give my work the concentration that it needed. Only then could I justify indulging myself in what I wanted to do.

This was not the life I was expecting or had planned. I am not sure that I had really planned anything when I was young. I was an army daughter and spent most of my childhood travelling and living abroad. I moved house ten times and had been to ten different schools before I was eleven. Then my parents parked me in a girls' boarding school in England. There was no sixth form at the school. Everyone left at sixteen. We learnt no science subjects. So-called 'finishing schools' or secretarial colleges were the further

education for most of us. Then it was marriage – some of my friends as early as nineteen.

For me, marriage happened at twenty-one and two children arrived a few years later. I spent many years squeezing in my work as best I could, first as an interior designer, and then as a counsellor with Marriage Guidance, in the intervals between looking after the children, running two houses, letting our flat to tenants, visiting elderly relations and entertaining friends, not to mention my husband's colleagues and students. During that time I also studied at the Open University. For a time, too, I was a school governor, a prison visitor and helped with an adult literacy programme.

Then, twenty years ago, my husband went freelance and I became his agent and manager, discovering, somewhat to his and my surprise, that I was rather good at it. Luckily, I have always enjoyed being busy, but it was my life as well as his, I felt, and that dormant passion for photography was beginning to surface. It was time to take it seriously. I bullied my way on to a part-time degree course and five years later found myself queuing up to look at the degree lists on the very day that our son was doing the same at his university. To our joint relief we both passed, with exactly the same class of degree. It doesn't matter when you do it, I reckoned then, if you want it enough you can always get it. I still believe that.

As I turned sixty, my first reaction was one of disbelief. Am I really sixty? Surely it cannot be me. Being sixty is what I associate with my mother – or my aunt – or someone else. But then I only have to look in the mirror or see a photograph of myself and the reality is there. Obviously I am no longer the young person that I think I am. I have bags under my eyes, a double chin and I am beginning to have the odd white hair.

I feel exasperated with my memory. I cannot remember names and places. People I can't even remember meeting tell me of deep conversations we have had. I start a new book and realise only near the end that I know how it's going to finish – because I had read it before. I cannot learn Italian despite endless tapes listened to, talked back to – and then forgotten. On the other hand I can remember every photograph I have ever taken! Funny that! We can remember what we want to remember.

I am saddened, too, by how many friends have died or have become seriously ill. As the funerals become more frequent I am made more conscious of my own death and also that of my husband. It is a jolt for a control freak like myself to take on board that the end of life is one thing that is not completely under my control.

On the other hand, looking back now at sixty, I can understand better where I have come from and why I am who I am. I am no longer angry with my parents. For much of my life I just wished they had been very different kinds of people. I understand, now, that they behaved in the way they did because of who they were. I am at peace with my past. Age, too, has made me less shy and more sure of myself. I no longer care what people think of me, nor who they are.

I feel now, at sixty-one, that I am in a stage of life where I can choose to do almost anything that I want to. We have a good life, my husband and I, still together and loving it, every part of it, after forty years. I know, however, that I should not count on this stage lasting for ever. Who knows for certain what is brewing inside us, or what accidents lie in wait? I worry only that there will not be enough of the sort of time we are now enjoying. Retirement is not an idea I can get my head around. As long as I can see something through my viewfinder, life will be worth living.

ALLEGRA TAYLOR

Life's tapestry

How do you combine the desire for a stable home and family with an insatiable wanderlust? Allegra Taylor explains how her writing made it possible and how it has prepared her for her sixties.

The first thing I did when I reached sixty, possibly more vain than wise, was to dye my hair red. After ten years of trying to age gracefully I abandoned the attempt with relief. The best thing about getting old is growing into oneself and not trying particularly to please anyone else.

At the age of sixty I ponder the meaning of happiness and wonder if it isn't merely the simple fact of being mindful of each precious day. Futile to mourn the should-have-beens; might-have-beens. Foolish to fear the future. Who knows if there'll be one? Today is all we ever have. Cancer gave me this invaluable perspective – a pleasing sense of the quiet spaciousness of being here now, alongside an acceptance of the immutable law of impermanence.

My chaotic childhood was a useful preparation for this new state of mind: the fact that sometimes we'd go to school in a taxi and at other times there'd be no money for shoes so we'd walk there barefoot or not go at all; the fact that my mum was a chicken farmer and my dad was a philosopher; the fact that we moved house every couple of years because the grass was greener in California or Brazil or Canada.

What held us together was a deeply instilled sense of specialness. Life was an adventure. My mother could make a home in a cheap hotel room with candles on the table, Brahms on the radio and a tin of Heinz spaghetti. My father told wondrous tales of a magic monkey. He made us laugh with Jewish jokes and showed me the rings round Saturn through a telescope. Mum kept the home together, got a job, paid the bills, found the piano teacher. Dad dreamed the dreams, gave me Dostoevsky to read and brought home carved elephants from India and bottles of Château Lafite. They were an incongruous pair. She a ravishing red-haired beauty from the crumbling, impoverished aristocracy; he a small, round Jewish refugee from Poland who lost all his family in the Holocaust. They loved each other madly, tempestuously.

'Have I ever told you', my father would say, 'that your mother is the most wonderful woman in the world?' He had. Many times. 'Your father is a genius,' my mother would confide, 'and one day he will write a masterpiece.' He never did but it didn't matter. They loved us and showed us that love was possible – the greatest gift of all. And even though we never had a proper home or stayed anywhere long enough to make friends – the family became the raft we all clung to. In retrospect I can see we were definitely odd – misfits in a world of normal people whose fathers mowed the lawn and whose mothers didn't sell eggs door to door in Beverly Hills.

The legacy of this unorthodox start was a burning desire to establish a still centre somewhere in my life, coupled with a profound need to gather up the little bitty fragments of my jigsaw – an incongruous mix of a longing for a stable home and an insatiable wanderlust.

Part one was satisfied by the enormous good fortune of meeting, at the age of sixteen, a very lovely man, a film maker, who has been my husband, my friend and my life's companion for the past forty-four years. Together we have raised six children – three home grown, adopted twins from Nigeria and an adopted daughter from Kenya. I am passionate about family and want, more than anything, to be the granny I never had. To date we have been blessed with twelve grandchildren. I love the truly international, multi-racial nature of our little tribe and hope that the sense of being loved that I was given has been passed on to them.

While our children were young I attempted to fill in some of the lamentable gaps in my own schooling and eventually achieved a London University B.Ed. degree with music as a special subject. For the next ten years I ran my own music school teaching piano and guitar to the neighbourhood children – a hugely enjoyable way to feel a part of the community. I was also learning how to write by doing magazine journalism.

As the children began to push off into the world, the need for a job that fitted around school holidays became less pressing and the writing began to take precedence. If I could get a book contract, I could plunge into a subject more deeply than an article gave scope for, I could travel and I could finance myself at the same time. I was nearly fifty and the subject with which I had become fascinated was healing. Were there links between ancient tribal forms of healing and the huge growth of interest in holistic health care and complementary medicine in the West?

The objective of the first book was to journey around the world to look for different manifestations of the 'healing encounter', apprenticing myself to healers, shamans, medicine people to try to arrive at a better understanding of the phenomenon.

My second book looked at the part that healing can play at the end of life. I wanted to confront the dreaded taboo, to think about my own mortality and that of the people I love, to become more skilful or at least less useless around the subject of death. I got a job working as a volunteer in a hospice and I joined London Lighthouse, the AIDS initiative, as a home support team member.

Everything I learned about healing helped me work with the dying. I learned that healing is not synonymous with cure, that people can be healed into death. One exceptional man with AIDS whom I met through my work at Lighthouse said to me, 'I realise that my illness presents me with a choice. Either to be a helpless, hapless victim dying of AIDS or to make my life right now what it always ought to have been.' And so he did, saying shortly before his peaceful death that he'd been able to make these changes because the loving care he'd received at Lighthouse had made him see himself in an entirely new light – as someone worthy of love.

I never forgot those words and when I had to deal with my own diagnosis of cancer and the irony of learning to put into practice my theories about healing and facing the possibility of death, they helped me enormously in making sense of the confusion. This theme was echoed again and again during the writing of my next book – on prostitution. This might seem to be a subject a million miles away from healing but it isn't. It is about wounded women trying to become whole. It is also about the very fine line between the healer and the whore; about the longing for warmth and love and human companionship.

This time I got a job as a maid in a brothel; making the tea, answering the phone, showing 'clients' into the waiting room, running a bath for the tired working women. In between clients we talked – about pregnancy, childbirth, miscarriages, children in hospital and the pain and loneliness of life when you only seem to give out but never seem to get much back. If healing is about bal-

ance and wholeness, the lives of most prostitutes are examples of bitter fragmentation.

My own healing journey of discovery and spiritual awakening brought me very close to the women I met in the course of writing that book. Helping them to form a support group sowed the seeds of the creative writing workshops which have become such an important part of my work in the past few years. As with all women, so much of our healing depends on our respect for and acceptance of each other just as we are. By sharing our stories we free ourselves from the hold they have over us.

And the journey continues. When the grandchildren started to arrive I set off on another quest – this time to meet wise old women around the world and to ask myself: What kind of old woman do I want to be? How do I learn to age with confidence and celebration in a culture that fears and denies getting older? How do other cultures do it? I stayed with an Apache cattle rancher in Arizona, a woman chief in the Cook Islands and an English village witch. These and other brilliant women became the inspiration for my book *Older Than Time – A Grandmother's Search for Wisdom*.

The most recent book *Ladder to the Moon – Women in Search of Spirituality* completes what I now can see as a quartet of archetypal themes: The Healer, The Whore, The Crone, The Priestess – aspects of the feminine that have become quite split off from one another – in which I have tried to gather up threads and weave a whole tapestry. In all my post-Twickenham-housewife travels I realise I have been collecting the different fragments of that scattered childhood.

And now, with one artificial hip joint, two mutilated breasts and ever stronger spectacles, I tango on into the sunset. A novel is brewing, I have a healing practice, I love to teach my writing work-shops and I have started going to salsa lessons. Whether I have a long life or a short one, I want to make today the best that it can be. I have been given the gift of knowing there is no time to waste.

ANITA RODDICK

On the threshold

*Success can be a prison – unless you
reinvent yourself, your relationships and your arenas.
Anita Roddick describes how she looks forward
to the challenge.*

've never been able to stand 'old' people, people for whom
ageing becomes an excuse for physical and mental inertia. Perhaps that's why my own attitude to ageing was a little ambiguous.
I relished the idea of accumulated wisdom but I was bothered by
the thought of ageing as some kind of ante-room to death, and
death has always been my bogeyman, to the point where I was
scared to sleep in case I never woke up.

If that suggests I might have what are popularly known as
'issues', I hasten to add my phobia was *then* and this is *now*. I'm
fifty-nine, looking at a door opening up to a new world. I'll admit
to a touch of trepidation but it is really exhilaration that I'm feeling. I think I'm not quite done yet with the business of being a

woman. You know, the whole thing of worrying about what you look like, how you're relating to people, what they're thinking of you. I hasten to add that I never look at a younger woman and wish I was her. I want to broker time, not looks. I believe that a door is opening on a decade when I'll celebrate everything that has come before in my life. I imagine the day must come when I'll look back and see that door closing, and I'm sure that will be a shock. But between then and now, I intend to have fun, *real* fun.

My life has been unorthodox. It couldn't have been any other way because I am my mother's daughter. Everything I am I can lay at the feet of Gilda, the woman who went hot-air ballooning in her eighties. I grew up in Littlehampton, which was about as twitchy-net-curtain as the south coast got, so you can only imagine how my mother, an impassioned Italian *paisana*, stood out. She drummed into me that I should be anything but mediocre. And she taught by example. For instance, my feelings about the inadequacies of organised religion were sealed by the sight of my mother hurling a bucket of dirty water at the parish priest when he came to talk to her about my father's funeral. That Italian peasant stock seemed to endow her with the best bullshit detector I've ever encountered.

It also seemed to heighten Gilda's flair for drama. She never had any sense of aesthetics, but boy, could she make a scene! I sometimes wonder if I've been running away from that all my life. On the other hand, her faith in the power of love has always been an inspiration for me. The man I knew as my Uncle Henry was the love of her life – and, as I found out later, my real father. When she managed to ditch her husband and marry Henry, their happiness was tragically short-lived, but the way she has carried him with her for the rest of her life has never ceased to move me. It's been a standard against which I measure the depth of my own emotions.

My mother taught me a number of other vital lessons that shaped my business. Her work ethic, for example, meant that her kids worked in her café as soon as they were able to carry a tray. I graduated to the coffee machine. Sure, it was tough, but I learned that you can bring your heart to work. I'm sure that's where my sense that values add value was formed. Gilda's waste-not-want-not attitude to life, sharpened by the rationing of the war years, also made her an environmentalist without even knowing it. In our house, necessity was always the mother of invention. So, in my first shop, I refilled bottles because I couldn't afford to buy any more, and what became the Body Shop's signature green was simply the colour that best covered damp spots on the wall of my little shop in Brighton. If she'd chosen to, I'm sure Gilda could have seen herself in all those small economies that later went on to be corporate hallmarks.

And then, of course, Gilda played matchmaker. She introduced me to Gordon Roddick. The evolution of a relationship – always assuming you can make it last – is one of the more intriguing aspects of ageing. I wonder at women who are relieved when their partner dies because it gives them a chance to re-create themselves. I would hope that my relationship with Gordon never stunted my growth in that way. That's because our relationship has always been a partnership. Admittedly, it's been highly unconventional. I opened a shop because I needed to support our daughters and myself while Gordon fulfilled his lifelong dream of travelling on horseback from Buenos Aires to New York. There were a lot of people who thought it was absolutely bizarre that I would accept such a thing, but we were never interested in being a couple who were joined at the hip. Our relationship has been based not on dominance and submission but on friendship and trust. And if that trust is ever shaken, don't we all just groan and move on?

I guess that's because you're not lost in passion at this age. You choose compassion over passion. It's less about sexual bliss than caring. Does that mean you reinvent partnership in your sixties? I hope so. Maybe it's true that the happiest unions are not the best behaved ones. Anyway, it's the debate, the challenge, the

anticipation of things you can do together I've always relished most. In that sense, your relationship with your partner becomes your relationship with the rest of the world. But I really wish there were more information about how you maintain a partnership at this age.

You always hear about the adventures and the excitements. You rarely hear about the unromantic aspects of marriage. Maybe that's because men are no longer the centre of women's lives when they reach their sixties. That's truer today than ever before. Women are finding new storylines. They're going it alone or living with younger, less accomplished men. They're not preoccupied with the issues that make an ageing man's life such a minefield. They have a new sense of liberation. Attraction, seduction – these words mean something else now.

I was always fascinated by my mother's relationship with my daughters. There was a natural intimacy that I never seemed to manage. But now I have my own granddaughters and suddenly it all starts to make sense. I'm part of a great female continuum, an eternal present. When I look at my granddaughters, I don't think about the future. Obviously, I hope they live fulfilled lives and come to the stage I'm at and feel there's nothing unrequited. But the thought of me being gone from their lives simply stops my breath.

My God! Are we back with that 'issue'? I think about the closest I've ever come to actual death, when I was in Sarawak trying to film the illegal logging of the rain forest. If we'd been discovered, we'd have been massacred. The terror of discovery was savagely acute, yet I had it in my mind that perhaps this was the way to die, while the rage was still burning inside. That suggests my spiritual journey has probably carried me about half an inch from my young self.

But then there was the Battle of Seattle, where I found myself literally in the tear-gassed and pepper-sprayed front line of the protests. I was re-radicalised. I realised that, even if I don't want to take physical risks any longer, the thrill of action and the discipline of commitment will always make my life more worthwhile. This is me at sixty – a woman who realises all those assumptions about age were someone else's hang-up; a visionary who has surprised herself with what she has become; an activist with a pragmatic awareness of how to make her vision a reality.

The idea of self-discovery is still a little too hoary for me. Gilda always talked about it as reinvention. As usual, she was right. I'm hungry for a new arena, a forum of ideas, where everything I've learned, everyone I've met can be brought into play. You know why? Because the play is the thing. That's one thing ageing truly teaches you. Your role will constantly change and you'll do yourself – and those around you – a hell of a favour if you just roll with those changes. When I think of Gilda in her hot air balloon, I realise it's still a long time till curtain call.

Behaving badly at sixty-five

Passion and pigs as a recipe for one's sixties?
Audrey Eyton, the best-selling author of The F-Plan
Diet, *explains how a discovered passion has given*
her purpose and fulfilment.

After moving to Canterbury, many years ago, I gradually formed an image of myself when old and still, from time to time, nostalgically glimpse the gracious figure that might have been. Daily, to the sound of summoning bells, she makes her stately way through the precincts and up the ancient steps to the cathedral's early-medieval choir. She wears a Queen Mary toque – black and veiled. 'Here comes Mrs Eyton,' they mutter respect-fully as she settles into her pew and the peace and tranquillity of Evensong. Naturally, it is the same seat in the same pew, which no one else would dare to occupy. The virtual old and stately Mrs Eyton of my mind's eye is a mite more formidable than my actual five foot two.

Little did she anticipate, poor dear, so swift a terminal decline. It started one evening, many years ago, during the final years of South Africa's apartheid system when Father Trevor Huddleston came to speak in Canterbury. The old campaigner was getting frail and rather crusty. It wasn't a wonderful speech. But suddenly, right at the end, the passion not evident in his earlier words poured out in a final plea for support for his cause: 'I'm getting old and I can't die until I see the end of apartheid,' he concluded. I was transfixed. Envious, even. A new image was born. What a wonderful reason for wanting to stay alive – to carry on fighting for something one cared about even more than life. How marvellous to be able to lose one's dental fillings but retain one's passion.

This new scenario for my old age continued to alternate for a time with that of the still not quite deceased but sadly ailing 'gracious' Mrs Eyton. Then my son Matthew stopped eating meat and all the unease for so long shoved down into my own subconscious surged to the surface. I had always known, as do we all, that most intensive farming systems involve great cruelty to animals. At some time, but not just yet, I would try to do something about it, I assured myself. But meanwhile I remained among the useless in the 'Don't tell me I can't bear to hear about it' brigade.

Suddenly, some time became now. I investigated intensive farming and wrote a book. From then on my future was not in question. Now, at sixty-five, in what a New York friend terms 'the springtime of my senility', I look back on my younger self as a different being. Just how late can a late developer be? Taking half a century to discover that the Western world is not run by wise, well-meaning and basically benevolent beings is ridiculous. Maybe I was always just too busy. The former Tory voter has turned into a radical rebel, prepared to carry a banner and join those at the cutting edge of change. I am rejecting the deeply ingrained morality of my society, even of the Church, and

actually thinking for myself. It's a heady feeling. I've discovered it's never too late to think.

To be fair to my old self, a gradual and barely noticed moral evolution was going on as I made my way up in journalism, started my own magazine – the first ever published on the subject of slimming – and enjoyed my fifteen minutes of fame as the author of a blockbusting best-seller, *The F-Plan Diet*. This change can be neatly encapsulated in my response to cowboy movies. As a child, at Saturday morning cinema, I cheered for the cowboys.

Later, having accepted society's changing ethics, I gradually shifted to the side of the Indians. Now my sympathies lie entirely with the cows.

Despite having more reasons than most to be sad, I have found my sixties to be the most fulfilling time of my life. My wonderful Matthew, so full of kindness and with a wit that often had me weeping with laughter, died at the age of twenty-four. My only other child had died as a baby. His father and I divorced in 1976. On Matthew's death I could contemplate no hope of future happiness but simply resolved to be useful, doubly useful for both of us, in the cause we shared. In that resolve I inadvertently found the secret of contentment. Happiness, I believe, is rarely if ever to be found from the seeking and comes only as an unexpected bi-product of other things. Things will never be the same since Matthew died but I strongly suspect my own contentment quota to be higher than that of many devoting their sixties to the pursuit of pleasure.

So what do I do? Good question. It's one I often ask myself. There are so many projects, so many strands, so many like-minded friends of all ages and nationalities whom I didn't even know ten years ago.

It all begins around eight o'clock each workday morning when I switch on my computer and log on to messages from fellow campaigners all over the world. There's saintly Louise, in South Africa, with news about the Humane Education project I fund in their schools, Gudrun in Hamburg with mailing queries and moans about her thirty-fifth failure to quit smoking, Glenys and Helen in Oz, as excited as I am at the latest order figures for the video they're helping me to promote, dear Richard, a deeply caring organic farmer from Warwickshire, updating me on our current research project. And many more . . .

The friends and contacts I have made in my fight against intensive farming are as diverse as the countries they live in. They range from bishops and scientists to cutting-edge anarchists. A battle for change and progress needs to be fought on many fronts. It always did.

The battle to change society's belief that only man matters is, and now will always remain, the core of my life. But friends and a little fun are necessary ingredients. Maybe because my work keeps me aware of what's happening in the world I find myself in tune with children of friends, my son's old school friends, and other young people as well as my own age group. They e-mail, telephone and come for weekends. 'My friends think it sounds rather dreary when I say I'm visiting my aunt,' my niece told me. 'They have no idea what fun we have.' I was pleased.

With my own generation of old friends and neighbours, few of whom share my beliefs, I think I've learned to be tactful. The battle for animal rights will not be won in the drawing rooms of Canterbury. I leave combat gear at home when I put on party clothes, mindful of that good old Northern expression 'save your breath to cool your porridge'.

Inevitably I have a few friends of the four-footed kind. There's my mongrel, Flyte, from an RSPCA rescue home, plus three sofa-sized pink pigs, which I somewhat inadvertently acquired.

It was never my intention to become a farm animal rescuer. I believe in fighting for the many, not saving the few. But when I took a crew to film pigs in intensive systems there was something about the pitiful frustration of Sow 206, gnawing the bars of her small stall, that just wouldn't shift from my mind. 'What's happened to 206?' I would enquire as casually as possible at the end of subsequent conversations. She was pregnant. She was about to give birth. She was – horrors – about to be slaughtered in two days' time. I cracked.

Suddenly I was engaged in a Hollywood-style death row drama, phoning, faxing and e-mailing to save her, begging and pleading to get someone to give her a home, weeping when the wretched woman who promised to do so let me down. Switch to final scene: Sow 206, Victoria as she has become, makes her stately way aloft a cart drawn down a country lane to take up permanent residence in a hastily fenced-off field on my own land. She lived there in perfect bliss for the next five years, foraging all day on roots, sweet chestnuts and acorns, wallowing in cooling mud in the heat, doing all the things that every factory-farmed pig longs to do, until her old legs gave out and, one beautiful summer evening, my vet put her gently to sleep as she contentedly munched Sainsbury's jam tarts.

Victoria needed company, of course. And having acquired one pig it's easy to acquire more – almost habit-forming. Now there are three: Lucy, Riley, who has certainly lived the 'life of', and (I'm afraid) Babe, so prosaically named because she was trained to accompany Joanna Lumley to Parliament in an animal welfare publicity stunt. Babe, who shared a home with a young animal behaviour scientist during her training period, was 'house-trained' to use her pig-litter tray by the age of five weeks, could sit to command at six and knocked spots off all twelve-week-old pups in all activities at a puppy training class when she was half their age. Yet our society is content to allow highly intelligent, playful animals like this to endure life on metal slats between concrete walls in the dubious cause of cheaper bacon. I mustn't get started . . .

These days I study the mores and mannerisms of the elderly out of keen self-interest, fumbling in handbags (guilty), searching for specs (my hobby), walking into the next room and forgetting why one did. I have learned to prefix my anecdotes with 'Please stop me if I've told you this before – repeatedly'.

But I can, and hope I always shall, plead 'Not Guilty' to the most negative and life-draining aspect of age: that terrible tendency to get more and more concerned about less and less. As old ladies of my acquaintance glaze over at the mention of anything further flung than the weeds in next door's garden or their own arthritic knee, I'm fuming at the World Trade Organisation whose ethics-free trading rules make it near impossible for any country to raise trade-related welfare standards for man or beast. I can't vote against the WTO. But I can and do enthusiastically support the young people who demonstrate against it. And if some of their tactics get a little over-exuberant . . . well, that's hardly going to figure among my first fifty-thousand most pressing worries. Goodness, what a shocking attitude. The prim eighteen-year-old I was does not approve and gracious old Mrs Eyton has collapsed senseless with horror in her pew. Tough.

BRENDA WEIR

What *really* matters

With a busy husband, four children and a
series of businesses and other organisations to run,
you can soon end up as what Brenda Weir describes
as a Universal-Coping-Machine. Come sixty, and after
a serious illness, why not invest in oneself
for a change?

When you are young, sixty is unimaginable. When you *are* sixty, it seems unbelievable! What has happened to all those years? Where did all those dreams and ambitions go? Does it matter? No. Not when I am having more fun now than I have had since my late teens. That is because I am healthy; and doing things to please *myself* at last; and because I have a wonderful family and many good friends.

I grew up in the England of the Fifties – the end of the war years and a time of frugality and rationing, the last of the 'stuffy' decades – very different from the lavish wastefulness so obvious today. I had a happy childhood; was sent to a posh boarding school, which I loathed for the way in which it stifled any individuality and

trained us only to be the wives of successful men; had a couple of secretarial jobs and then, at the age of twenty-one, married a conservative Irish doctor. Somehow the dreams of being independent, unorthodox, a linguist, a pianist, a traveller had just evaporated; instead I went to live in southern Ireland and entered a time warp of at least thirty years earlier. Married women had no independent status – it was civil death. A woman's place was quite definitely in the home and my attempts to work were regarded with genuine astonishment by my in-laws.

It fell to my lot to sort out a confusion of family financial, legal and property matters, which was an unrewarded, time-

consuming and uphill task dealing with the (Irish male) account-
ants, bankers and legal people who plainly felt it was bizarre in the
extreme to be talking to a young woman about such things. But I
learned a lot, which was invaluable when I founded and ran a
small property company early on. To make friends in the rather
'cliquey' Irish scene I joined various voluntary committees –
mainly concerned with the conservation or restoration of a property, as I had always been interested in history and society. In the
process, I discovered a great talent for organisation, as well as an
unexpected delight in gardens and garden design, and a particular
joy in trees, which I planted around our dilapidated Georgian
home that was slowly being restored.

Four children (including twins) came along very quickly and
I was invited to found and run the association (formerly HITHA)
that is now known in Ireland as Heritage Properties (Stately
Homes etc. open to the public), which I am glad to say is still going
from strength to strength. I did my A levels by correspondence
course and went to university as a mature student. Then I ran a
small incoming travel company; I had lots of energy in those days!
Everything was done from home, of course, as it all had to be
worked around The Family which was – and still is – the most
important thing to me. Later on I even had a (disastrous) time
owning an Academy of Interior Design; and now I have emerged
from all this with a tiny business publishing a quarterly direct mail
newsletter called *Inside Ireland*, which is distributed primarily in
the United States of America – I've been doing that for twenty-five
years now and one of my daughters helps me with it.

No one reaches this age of sixty without experiencing
bereavement, betrayal, disappointment, disillusionment, sorrow
and the inevitable crises that have to be dealt with throughout life,
together with the anguish, distress, fury, bitterness and pain that
accompany these things. I have certainly had my fair share of all
that. Fortunately I am of an optimistic disposition, so even in the

darkest days of personal, family, marital, financial and health problems I rarely despaired completely, and coming to terms with all the ups and downs revealed to me a strength, resilience and sticking power that I did not know I had.

I know I have changed from being an intelligent, pretty, lively, impatient (and slightly bossy) personality to a much more tolerant, observant, understanding, thoughtful – indeed, rather boringly silent – and accepting person. Yes, of course I still feel impatient at times but I try to hide it! I have lived my life on two small islands, and I wish I had had wider experience. Here in Ireland the family and home have been absolutely central to my life, but if things had been different and I could have devoted more time and energy to my own aims, I think I could have been quite a successful businesswoman and I regret that my talents in that direction were never fully used.

I would love to have fluency in several languages and that will never happen now. But I am fortunate that I have lived for forty years in a lovely (at last fully restored) house and have seen my garden and trees grow and develop. I have wonderful children and am so proud of them. I am married (as my school promised) to a Man at the Top of His Profession. And I am enjoying the fruits of the hard-work years as I encounter the joys of grannydom – seven grandchildren so far and more to come, I hope!

A fun side of the sixties is the visible/invisible aspect. If you go out by yourself, carelessly dressed, hair windblown, no make-up – you know the sort of thing – and act in a generally 'older' way, no one will give you a second glance and you will rarely be remembered by anyone you meet. Waiters will put you in a corner, shop assistants think you can be overlooked and so on . . . It can be quite useful at times! But, of course, if you wish to become visible you have all the necessary confidence to command attention when you wish it. And to make a Big Impression, smarten up a bit and put on a hat! I remember years ago just after the war there was an advertisement that said, 'A hat made All the Difference'. It's quite true!

A few years ago I was gravely ill, so these are bonus years, and I am determined to enjoy them come what may. From being the buttress to the family and a sort of Universal-Coping-Machine, I found myself helpless in hospital. I was absolutely overwhelmed by the kindness and helpfulness of everyone. It taught me how necessary it is to 'let go'. Having the fragility of life brought so close alters one's focus: essentials are speedily sorted from the inessentials. There is no time and less point in resenting, reproaching and anticipating things 'that might happen'. Forgiveness of yourself and others is crucial so you can become comfortable with yourself. Don't feel guilty about pleasing yourself – and *do it now*! Never put off until later the things you want to do and the loving words you want to say.

So I'm really a New Woman. At long last I can travel – my newsletter enables me to go regularly to the USA, whence I return feeling young, thin and re-energised! And I visit family and friends abroad when I can. I am passionately fond of opera and interested in garden design, so those two things are the foundation for short trips, sometimes with a few women friends. We have a wonderful time doing vaguely cultural things, eating well and above all having a great laugh. And I enjoy lunching – both out with friends and entertaining at home. Friends are so important. I still tend to look at property with a speculative eye and again have a tiny involvement with that; but what is really important is *family*, *friends* and *fun*.

The future? Well, I am learning to play Bridge (useful now and for my old age, I am assured). I must become more computer-literate, learn to work the video and make use of my mobile phone (which everyone insists I must have). I'm just not a techie so all that will probably take me the rest of my days . . .

CAMILLA PANUFNIK

Merry? widow

*How do you rebuild your life when the centre
of it, the man around whom it revolved, has died?
Camilla Panufnik describes her experience of life
with and after Andrzej.*

In my early twenties I tumbled desperately in love with a man double my years but young in intellectual curiosity and with extraordinary good looks. Widowhood never entered my mind and we had almost thirty wonderful years together.

Andrzej Panufnik had slanting cheekbones and brown, hypnotic eyes. He had charm, courtesy, brilliance and a wicked sense of humour. He composed powerful, spiritual music. He was often stormy, never boring. Early in our acquaintance he quoted the Polish proverb: 'the way to a man's stomach is down his throat!' and claimed he married me for my cooking (though it was not very good in those early days). Andrzej was a political exile from Poland, who had made a dramatic flight to England in 1954 to tell the world of the plight of Polish artists under Stalinism. He had been through hell in Warsaw during the war. Then, as Poland's leading composer and conductor, he was bullied and criticised and politically exploited. He had a dismal first marriage, his adored six-month-old daughter died accidentally, and his parents and only brother were all dead. In England as an exile he eventually rejected the glossy life of the conductor in order to dedicate himself to composing. When we met, he had already decided never to marry again. My wait was worthwhile.

We had many good friends, especially in the music world. Legendary artists who had supper in our kitchen included Leopold Stokowski, Yehudi Menuhin, Georg Solti, Nadia Boulanger and many others. We went to friends' concerts, but otherwise eschewed social life.

It is a great privilege to make a man happy when he has endured fifty years of tragedies. I basked in his smile. I almost killed myself to cook to his utter pleasure. I reckoned that I was turning wifing into a transitive verb. We both worked incredibly hard because we enjoyed passionately what we were doing. Sometimes, as well as my books, I wrote verses for his cantatas and helped him with his programme notes. He liked to say his first language was music. He was excoriating about the modern expectation that composers should talk or write about their music, a pastime, he said, for those who had nothing to express between the staves.

I wanted to learn Polish. However, Andrzej, preferring to improve his eccentric English and pessimistic about the continued Communist domination of Poland, didn't want to be bored by my stuttering static phrases in his grammatically unfathomable mother tongue. I persisted for a while, but one day before a theatre performance he tested my comprehension. What he said was, 'The old woman next to me stinks like a rotten fish.' I didn't understand – but she, poor woman, got up and moved to another seat. He never spoke Polish to me again.

Our domestic peace was spasmodically interrupted with hectic trips around the Western world for premières of new compositions, concerts and recordings. Then we would return again to our gentle eighteenth-century home on the River Thames at Twickenham. We were blessed with two amiable, entertaining and naturally creative children. The house was like a factory. Andrzej was writing symphonies and concertos, I was producing photographic story books for children and more earnest publications for adults. Jeremy, who could draw almost from the day he could hold a pencil, made us laugh with his hilarious cartoons. He is now an able percussionist and succeeds both as artist and composer (and DJ). Roxanna was learning six different instruments and improvising her own music. She is now a celebrated young composer with her own harmonic language.

Like any family we had downs and ups – plenty of downs professionally in the dangerously competitive music business, with the added difficulties of fanatic musical fashions and the animosity of the political powers in Andrzej's native land. However, the ethic of hard work and our miraculous house and garden always kept us on course. Gradually things looked up and up, and, in 1991, he became the first naturalised Pole to gain a knighthood (for his services to music). Ever modest, he was so surprised; he first thought the envelope from 10 Downing Street was a joke.

Andrzej never looked or felt his age. I thought he would live to a hundred. Then cancer struck.

I was saved from self-destruction by my closeness to Roxanna and Jeremy, then still students, both as shattered as I was; also by my wonderful friends and clannishly devoted family; and, in the long run, by my hyperactive tendencies and a habit of happiness. But Andrzej had been the core of my life, my *raison d'être*.

I have now many widow friends and know after bereavement those first years pass terrifyingly slowly. In my case I couldn't just vanish and lick my wounds. Being married to an international composer, there were memorial concerts everywhere. In retrospect they were comforting, but Andrzej's familiar music, especially then, was like hearing his voice. Roxanna and I used to sit in the dark concert halls with tears tumbling down our faces while Jeremy bravely passed us more handkerchiefs. Even now certain of Andrzej's works make me dissolve.

The need to continue to cope with letters from publishers, recording firms and the like helped me towards a gradual gathering of my wits. I couldn't do my own work at all, but anyway Andrzej's had always taken precedence. At least it was no shock to have to cope with finances: Andrzej, completely uninterested in money, had always (unwisely) left business matters to me, resulting in a diminutive income but a huge benefit to his output as a composer. After his death I found bundles of unopened bank statements in his desk.

In Andrzej's last year, after the fall of the Wall and the restoration of Polish democracy, Andrzej, still a profound patriot after thirty-seven years of exile, finally returned to Warsaw. The Poles are wonderfully warm and emotional people. We were met as we came down the steps of the plane, by crowds on the tarmac carrying roses and with a band playing his Fanfare. There were standing ovations at his concerts. After his death the surging interest continued in Poland.

I realised that I would, belatedly, have to learn the language. Colloquial tapes in the car were valuable – the repetition helped both pronunciation and my appalling memory. Saintly and engaging instruction has also come from Andrzej's friend, the poet and professor, Jerzy Peterkiewicz. It is awesome to be taught by the official translator of the Pope's poems and author of books in both languages. And now, with the help of a dictionary which became elephant-eared rather than just dog-eared, I have managed to read the excellent new Polish biography of my husband, musicological terms and all.

If only that were all I had to do! I am pulled in all directions by my own professions and by a fascinating but demanding panoply of voluntary work. I loathe committees but am a soft touch when asked for help. And I am appalled to admit that I am on the boards or advisory councils of two theatres (in two countries), two orchestras, two organisations for young musicians, and two trusts. I seem to be patron of a dozen or so extremely worthy causes, president of three. None of these situations has been sought by me, and I refuse many requests, because there is no point unless I can be of positive and real help. I loathe fundraising unless I can use my professional skills as a writer or photographer to report on action in the field.

Not everything I do concerns music. In Vietnam and Cambodia, I was asked to photograph young landmine victims with missing limbs. There are landmines everywhere in these countries (also in Bosnia, which I visited recently), vicious, indestructible objects scattered in their tens of thousands, which will continue to explode a hundred years into the future.

There is sadness in this country too. This year I started up a volunteer project in our little local hospital for elderly neurological clients. Some of them are on the edge of Alzheimer's, unable to cope at home, institutionalised and bewildered. Some have no visitors at all. Our volunteer team is looking for Befrienders who will adopt an individual for at least one or two hours a week. There is so much to be done. I wish many more people would volunteer.

That makes me sound earnest. On the contrary, most evenings I'm out and about in London. My kind and amusing friends ensure my survival, and most of them share my passion for opera, music and all the arts. My adorable son and daughter live close by and – new phase – I have recently acquired not only a large, friendly son-in-law, but also an exquisite, diminutive granddaughter.

I still have a huge hole in my life but I'm blessed with a capacity for contentment. I haven't married again. Near misses have been tempting, but I always became boringly entangled in my own or the suitor's past-life baggage. Freedom to abandon home, guiltlessly to go anywhere I want when I want, is a stimulating alternative. Meanwhile between journeys I am absorbed in beaming hundred per cent attention into each action of the moment. I don't think about being sixty years old. But I do need sixty hours in every twenty-four.

CAROLE STONE

Friends galore!

We are each our mother's child, but few will enter their sixties so proudly proclaiming their mother's influence on their life and career as Carole Stone. She explains here how a shy child ended up at sixty as the queen of networkers, with over 16,000 names in her personal database. Carole was nearly sixty before she got married for the first time.

I'm a bit of a drama queen, but I've spent years hoping that one day, when I'm gone, my friends will say 'she took life in her stride'.

I want that epitaph so much because that's the way my darling mother lived. She was my inspiration. With courage and with optimism she took life by the scruff of the neck and dealt with it. She made me feel I could do anything in the world that I wanted to do, and yet she always gave me the freedom to fail. It was the 'having a go' that was so important to her – as now it is to me.

I'd always assumed that I'd marry young, have half a dozen children and live in the country, but the fact is nobody ever asked

me to marry them. I was mostly on my own, or anguishing over some elusive man, until at forty-six I met the television journalist, Richard Lindley. He kept me waiting ten years before proposing and when he did I wasn't quite sure whether to accept. I'd got as far as this on my own, why did I need a husband now? Wouldn't it cramp my style? But I'm glad now that I became a June bride when I was fifty-seven.

Marriage has made a big difference. It's made me feel anchored and even closer to Richard, without taking anything away from my sense of independence. Had I married earlier I might well have had children of my own, but I certainly wouldn't have been able to make the most of the opportunities I had to make the friends that are still so much part of my life today.

Today I earn my living bringing together people from the worlds of business, politics and the media who might otherwise never meet. It's something I'd go on doing for nothing even if I had enough money to live on without it. I get huge pleasure from putting people together and making them feel at ease. I have over 16,000 names on my personal database and a great many of them are much more than just contacts or even acquaintances. I'm astonished at how many of the people I meet, some extremely well-known and successful in their field, still feel at a loss when it comes to getting to know strangers.

I was not promising raw material to start with. Life handed me a big nose, small boobs, big feet and a rather coarse voice. On top of that I was painfully shy. But, with my mother's encouragement, I learned to make the friends that have been my solace and salvation in life.

I may have been a shy child, but my older brother, Roger, was pathologically so. He was later diagnosed as suffering from paranoid schizophrenia – his moods changed suddenly and he could be violent. It was frightening for all of us. But I think it was Roger's utter inability to communicate that made me more determined than normal to make friends and bring other people into our small family unit. It helped relieve the tension at home, where Mama worked exhaustingly long hours running a small sweet shop. And Dada, a former sergeant and champion boxer in the regular army, was all too often at odds with Roger.

When I left secretarial college I spent a couple of months in London 'temping' by day and attending a Lucy Clayton Charm course two nights a week. I wasn't sure what job I wanted, but Mama thought it would be a good idea for me to be well turned out! In fact, at twenty-one I became a copy typist in the newsroom of the BBC in Southampton. It was the beginning of a BBC career that ended with my running Radio 4's flagship programme *Any Questions?* for ten years.

Mama passed on to me her deep interest in people and how they live their lives. At the BBC I was in my element and throughout my years there I discovered that, no matter what their background, people all have the same worries and need the same things to make them happy. More than that, I realised that quite different people, when thrown together like my *Any Questions?* guests, soon find ways to get on with each other.

I was so eager for Mama to meet the people I was beginning to make my friends, and so wanted them to have the pleasure of meeting her, that I began holding little gatherings in my flat. Mama would move round the room, her eyes alight with pleasure, holding out her hand and saying proudly, 'I'm Kathleen, I'm Carole's mother.'

Those early drinks 'dos' gradually grew into my annual Christmas party. These days I welcome well over a thousand of my friends – it's a big event – but it still, I hope, retains its old warmth and family atmosphere.

Recently I began holding a 'salon' in my London flat – it sounds grand, but it's just a regular gathering of my friends, and sometimes their friends too, for a glass of wine and good conversation. The thing that makes it work is that it's at the same time, at the same place, on a regular date. My friends just give me a call if they are free to join me.

In my early fifties, when I'd left the BBC and was working as a freelance media consultant in London, Mama came to live in my Covent Garden flat. My father, my brother and my stepfather had all died, and as for me, Mama felt that I was now safely in Richard's loving care. 'I'm just Kathleen for the first time in my life,' she said. 'I'm no one's daughter, wife or mother, I'm me.' She felt free and full of hope. Yet she knew she was unwell. She'd smoked most of her life – whenever we were about to settle down for a cosy chat, she'd say 'Hold on a minute, dear' and rummage around for a cigarette before she was ready for serious conversation. In those six months she was with me in London we had the luxury to talk and talk – about all the things that mattered deeply to us.

I knew she was preparing me for her death.

One morning, on an impulse, we set off to shop for some shoes. We hailed a taxi and stepped inside. As we drove off, Mama suddenly took my hand in hers. 'I feel dizzy,' she said. 'Do you know, sweetheart, I think I'm going to faint.' She squeezed my hand and died.

I miss her all the while.

Mama had to turn down the chance of university because her family needed her wages. Had she been born twenty years later, I feel sure she'd have had a successful career – maybe as a journalist or even an academic. But Mama never dwelt on 'if onlys'. She'd married two men who both adored her, she'd made sure her son lived as happy a life as possible and she knew she'd been my inspiration – though she'd never in any way tried to live through me.

In my early life my mother helped me overcome my shyness. She showed me how to take an interest in other people's lives and to learn from them how to conquer my own problems. It is true to say, now, that learning the art of making friends has transformed my life. It's an added bonus that from time to time I feel these connections really have made a difference to other people's lives.

Now, as I enter my sixties, I think Mama has left me a legacy that's just as important: her attitude of mind. It's about continuing your journey, always looking around the corner of life, not in fear of what might be heading your way, but with optimism, welcoming something new – knowing that, whatever comes, you'll cope.

So now I'm ready to move on. I've written a book – *Networking – the art of making friends* – to show that you don't have to be born with money, social status, brilliant brains or conventional beauty to make the people you meet your friends. And, because I find friends so important a part of my life, I'm looking into the possibility of starting a members' club, where I hope I will be able to meet and make even more of them.

I think Mama would approve. I can almost hear her calm voice now, urging me forward. She'd like me to have a go.

CATHERINE WARNER

Young again at sixty

*Life can seem bleak after your marriage
breaks down in your late fifties, but there can be a
new life waiting, as Catherine Warner explains.*

It is more than four years now since I gave up my life as a company wife with the man I had known since I was eight years old.
He was not well, but was much more seriously ill than I realised. I
am still coming to terms with what happened and as time goes by
my understanding of the situation changes but clarifies. I did find
out that very few people have the ability to stand back and view
such dramatic change with patience.

How lucky I have been! At my lowest point I met someone
who wanted to help, someone who had valued his lost family life
and who offered me a strong and steady hand. We have now
been married for two years. I am sixty-one, retired and very
comfortable after forty years of home building, career chasing
and accumulating goods and chattels. For different reasons both

my husband and I have given up our family homes, all gone –
broken up!

So where and how do we live now?

Two small houses – one in the Docklands in London, with
Jubilee, District and Circle lines ten minutes away, and one at
Bredon Hill in the country. We have theatres, galleries, museums,
opera and ballet. Then there is the country garden, which I love
and at present am redesigning. There are hill walking, riding,
Stratford, Cheltenham and Malvern all nearby – and all these
things to enjoy with friends and family. I read quite a lot, but
much slower now, as I have to struggle with my changing eyesight. We both enjoy finding good quality food. My husband is a
more serious cook than I so I benefit from his high standards in
the kitchen.

And how do we apportion our 365 days each year?

My daughter lives in Switzerland with her family of three, my
son in New Zealand with his family of two. There is another step-
granddaughter in Shropshire and a stepdaughter and grandson in
Sheffield. My mother is eighty-one and lives alone in Lancashire.
So visiting family and friends takes up about one-third of the year
along with holidays and travel. The rest of the time we divide
between London and the country. This perpetual-motion lifestyle
looks quite glamorous to our young, who are all busy bringing up
their families and climbing their respective career ladders.

I remind them that we were the generation who married
young, no living together for us, and of course the advantages are
now apparent. Yes, we had to struggle in our twenties, no waiting
for the right job, the car and the spending power. But having
turned sixty, I have a lovely mother, who is great-grandma to five
and step-grandma to two. I still enjoy sewing, knitting, gardening,
serious walking and scuba diving. Many of these activities we do
with our family. I ski, ride and rollerblade with the grandchildren;
sailing will soon be another of our sports as the older ones have

started lessons. One of my very greatest joys is to holiday with the family and see my mother play with my children's children.

It has been a long time coming.

My father was a policeman during the war and later became a teacher. The forties and fifties were very tough by today's standards especially in the North. I was brought up to understand that the depression was a terrible and shaming thing and that financial security was extremely important. I might have had an artistic career if I had been thirty years younger, but the security and pension offered by the teaching profession seemed the only acceptable course to take and my father made sure I understood this.

By the time I was twenty-three, I had begun my career in teaching, had married and, with two small children, a dog and a green mini car, we were launching ourselves on life. My teaching career went on for twenty-one almost unbroken years. After nine years I moved into special education and, having completed a year's extra study, I taught severely physically disabled children. The work was very demanding, but very rewarding. My children got on well at school and my husband's career went well. My husband's career always came first and he had my full support. Then, in the early eighties, he had an important career move to the North of England just as both children went to university and our London-based life was exchanged rather unwillingly for life in the North again.

I stopped my teaching career at this point. At the age of forty-three I redesigned my life by becoming not only a good company wife, but also a Pennine hill farmer. With no experience except the occasional TV programme of *The Good Life*, I plunged into an unknown world. Stalwart Yorkshire farmers grinned sceptically at my efforts, I read the books, wielded the pick and shovel, built up broken walls, chased unruly animals across the moors and worked from dawn until dusk. So much to learn because it was not a hobby. I wanted my beef to be the best, my lambs to bring the highest prices, my hay to be the sweetest and the tastiest, and I knew that respect from the local farming community would only be given when it was truly deserved. My hands grew rough, my shoulders broad and the feeling of liberation and achievement was a constant driving force. I felt deeply fulfilled.

The farming went well and, since I knew that age would slow me down, I began to plan my future. I would plant mixed woodland, cut down on the stock and contribute to the well-being of the countryside by tending trees all around the old farmhouse. Of course, life does not usually follow the pattern of one's dreams and, after ten years, I had to steel myself to sell everything in order to follow my husband and his career to another location.

There were tears, despair and emptiness – but stiff upper lip, face the new life and all that… By this time our accountant daughter was married and living near Oxford. Our son was working for WHO in the South Pacific islands as a doctor, and something was quite wrong in my marriage. During the moving period forty-ton trucks on motorways twice crashed into me from behind, without warning. The second time there was a serious pile-up with instant deaths. My car was a write-off and I became very ill and confused.

No amount of 'Have a gin and tonic and pull yourself together', 'Go to Caroline' (my daughter), 'Have a breakdown', 'Spend money' did any good. After counselling I did seem to improve, but inside I was looking for the bus to walk in front of, or the motorway bridge to drive into. I had hundreds of aspirins hidden away and I became very frightened when I realised that I was on a downward spiral, out of control. The world around me was full of happy, apparently normal people and they all seemed a million miles away even when I was in their midst. Just a few friends saw a serious problem. My mother was not at all surprised when I loaded the car and ran away. Neither were the children.

My grandparents could never have understood what I did and I imagine that my own father, had he been alive, would have been truly ashamed of me. They all did the decent thing, and slid into old age with determination and grace at the appointed time. The trials and ordeals of life never got the better of them.

I am glad I brought my children up in a Christian and united family. I am sorry that I grew apart from my husband when the children left home. He loved his career and I think it killed him. The fact that I was not there for him until the end is something that I alone have to live with. I had to go, it was a compulsion. I had to find my lost self, I truly had lost my grip and I needed to fight hard to regain my stability and take charge of the rest of my life.

Life is full again, with my new husband. Together we laugh, we talk, we argue, we love our own and each other's families and most of all we love each other. We have to tread carefully with our children. This love thing in the over-sixties is hard for them to understand, while we think our inner sixteen-year-old emotions are well tempered by our ages. My dear friend Rene always said, when her children were being disruptive, 'You can't put an old head on young shoulders.' But I now know for certain that under my old head are some very young shoulders indeed.

CLAIRE EVANS

Confessions of a divaholic

*How and why does a diplomat's wife end up
as a part-time opera producer and singer, as well as
a hopeful jazz clarinettist, in her sixties? Claire Evans
explains all and concludes that nothing
is impossible if you want it enough.*

There's a chance remark by Figaro to Cherubino in Mozart's *Marriage of Figaro* (when the randy lad is commanded by the jealous Count to leave for the army) which goes, 'Come cangia in un punto il tuo destino,' which roughly translated runs, 'How just one chance moment can change your destiny!' Looking back, I've always felt this was true of how the operatic enterprise started for me. We were living in Rome, where my husband was Agricultural Attaché with the embassy. Every year FAO (the Food and Agricultural Organisation, whose choir we had joined) would put on a musical and my particular 'life-changing moment' came when the juvenile lead in *White Horse Inn* had a nervous collapse just a fortnight before their annual production was due to take to the boards. Experienced replacement talent was unavailable at such short notice, so I found myself, very much a middle-aged compromise candidate, catapulted into the role, frenetically learning my part, spoken and sung, trying on costumes and getting my mind round the terrifying experience of my theatrical début. After a week of performances I was a convert – and, like most converts, the obsession has stuck.

How had I, a Yorkshire lass, ended up here? I was born in a rush in a Harrogate nursing home in March 1941, and grew up in the Yorkshire Dales where I was schooled until aged nine in the lee of Ilkley Moor. Boarding school followed, and a year of travels around the world. Then a secretarial course and an array of varied jobs, including working for Robert Maxwell at the Pergamon Press, Mallets the antique dealers and the Italian Institute of Culture in London. In 1965 I married Birnie and moved with him to Milan, then to Brussels and Algeria, and finally back to Oxford. I had just got the offer of a paid job with Oxfam there when the suitcases were out again after my husband accepted the job as Agricultural Attaché at the embassy in Rome.

I suppose being brought up to consider my role in life to be an adjunct to a husband rather than an initiator in my own right meant that the step from participant to perpetrator was mentally a steep one, but the Roman villa (modelled on one in Herculaneum) in which we lived with our ten-year-old daughter was just clamouring for a performance. It was built round a three-sided courtyard with a pillared loggia opening on to exquisite Mediterranean pine woods, and I knew it was there that we had to stage a mini-version of Monteverdi's *Poppea*. So this is just what we did, on a balmy night in midsummer with friends gathered round a central pool afloat with candles, a mixed band of early and present-day instruments, and a conductor who had only arrived in Rome the previous week.

This surprisingly successful foray led, two years later, to a much-reduced version of the *Marriage of Figaro* with string quartet and harpsichord – this time in the two-storey sitting room of our villa, into which we crammed ninety people. The main drama paled into insignificance when an overenthusiastic small child momentarily got her head stuck between the banisters. We added to the tension, during the love duet between the Count and Susanna, by having to scale a large pine chest inadvertently abandoned in the only entrance.

Later, with more experience, the now established company staged several performances of Rossini's *L'occasione fa il ladro* (*Opportunity Makes the Thief*) in two lovely Roman settings. The first was the British School at Rome (principally an art and architecture college) where we performed in a jasmine-scented courtyard with central fountain and two large cypresses between us and the orchestra. This necessitated two conductors, one for the instrumentalists and one for the singers!

The second setting for the Rossini was the residence of the ambassador to the Holy See, a lovely house on the southern stretch of the old Roman walls near the Porta di San Sebastiano. The performance was enlivened, during my second-act solo, by a tipsy carabiniere lurching on to the stage in full ceremonial uniform and clanking spurs after some excessive wine-bibbing during the interval. For similar reasons our leading soprano set off, unaccompanied, on a stretch of her Act One recitative halfway through Act Two. No wonder our performances have such an enthusiastic following.

The disappointment of leaving Rome for Oxford after eight years had been much mitigated by discovering that our first conductor and his singer wife, Alasdair and Rosy Jamieson, were living just down the road. Such a miraculous coincidence led to the production of three small operas, all under Alasdair's baton. These were staged at the Unicorn Theatre, Abingdon, a little gem formed from the remains of the Abbey buildings with a tiny theatre and a long medieval gallery perfect for post-performance festivities. The last two productions had an afterlife too – in Italy.

Prior to my husband's retirement in 1991, we had bought a derelict farmhouse in Umbria, which we have since renovated with huge angst and expense. We took the operas out there, lock, stock and barrel, giving two open-air performances, and living together – cast, instrumentalists and helpers – in great and crowded happiness for a week prior to the shows. Fearful, too, lest the diet of bricks and mortar should deaden the brain, I set off on the quest for the degree I had missed out on and am now four and a half years into an Open University Course, mainly in Music. We now spend our time between Oxford and Umbria, where we produce our own olives and make our own terrible wine, and where I am just embarking on the next opera production, as well as learning to play the clarinet, hopefully with a future in a jazz band.

The next opera will be the seventh production of our Shoestring Opera – and the name means what it says. No participant is paid; I try to hire theatre and scores as reasonably as possible; and the costumes and sets are assembled through the genius and invention of enthusiastic friends and a long-suffering husband. The group has three criteria: one, all participants should enjoy themselves; two, it should aim to give pleasure to its audience; and three, each performance should be followed by a party. If, in so doing, it can raise money for its chosen charity, then so much the better.

About a month before each production, I wonder how I ever voluntarily got embroiled in such a taxing and hare-brained enterprise, and how my poor family will survive the resultant ups and downs. Yet the seeds of such musical insanity were planted early on. From the time during the war when my Scots grandpa dandled me as a toddler on his knee, strumming out 'The Bluebells of Scotland' or 'I'll tak' the Hi' Road' on our old upright, through my

childish tears on first hearing Gigli sing 'Torna a Sorrento' until my determination, after my first concert (aged five), to play the harp, music must have been permeating my bloodstream. My enlightened parents took me to my first opera – *Il Seraglio* – aged fourteen. Music continued with a job in a London antique shop taking very much second place to queuing in the early morning for tickets to the Covent Garden gods, and the delightful coincidence of living in a flat right above Joan Sutherland and Richard Bonynge, and listening to her warming up and practising the best bits from my favourite operas.

So music has been seminal for me. Added to this, from the time I was 'finished' in Florence, aged eighteen, comes a deep-seated love of Italy, the smell of resin from the pines in the hot sun, the grey-green froth of olive trees in the breeze and the full-blooded verve of Italian singers. Together with painting and colour and language, all these elements seem to combine perfectly in an operatic production – but, looking back, what is perhaps more important than anything is the stamina to overcome the inevitable crises of a production and the confidence to carry it through to a finished product.

If I had had the confidence when I was younger, then I might not now, aged sixty this year, be setting off on yet another production like some confirmed alcoholic. Confidence came late and is difficult to acquire at will. I feel it has something to do with setting oneself realistic targets (just within reach), and tackling and building on them with dogged determination. It is certainly true that every production is yet another hurdle to be overcome in the never-satisfied quest for an ephemeral perfection. However, in the midst of all the anxieties of staging and singing in a performance, I often think back to how important it is to take that 'chance moment' to change direction when it comes, and to be prepared to say 'yes' and give the opportunity time to take flight. I know that despite all the difficulties I'm still glad I decided 'to tak' the hi' road' – even if I did start a bit late.

DIANA SHARPE

Legal gadfly in a Suffolk garden

*Not many would think of helping to start
an international law firm as they turned sixty.
Diana Sharpe did.*

I am sixty-nine. I feel happier, more fulfilled, more stimulated and more contented than ever before in my life. Apart from a slightly creaking knee, I feel better than I did at twenty – or thirty – or forty . . . And it all came together after my sixtieth birthday.

I was an only child. My mother was intelligent and organised. She had been a nursing sister and worked again during the war when I went to boarding school. She would have liked a longer career but my father developed MS so she devoted herself to him instead. Our relationship was distant and rather wary.

I loved my father, at a distance, but totally adored my grand-father who took time to nurture his 'little woman' and introduce her to books and music and the countryside. He never spoke ill of a soul.

I enjoyed my schooldays, found studying easy and managed a scholarship to Oxford. My parents were thrilled and proud, and made plans for my future. Then I delivered the bombshell. I would not go to university . . . I wanted to be an actress! Shock, horror! They were appalled. They insisted that I must take this chance to make a proper career – the kind of career my mother never had. There was a family stand-off and an immediate summer job in a factory at my father's insistence, to bring me to my senses. There I met women with hearts of gold and language which would have taken paint off doors. Quite an eye and ear opener for a convent girl!

I never did go to Oxford. I went to London instead, to be a nurse at Bart's. I learned a lot more than I bargained for – not only how to poach an egg and mitre corners, care for patients and keep a tidy linen cupboard, but how to plan ahead, prepare for contingencies, organise a work team and manage my time.

I went to New York to do some post-qualification training. There I fell in love and intended to stay for ever, but the romance fell foul of family prejudices so I took a summer job at a children's camp in the Adirondacks to gather my forces and decide what to do next. It was very near a summer stock theatre company, which was like a flame to a moth. I spent most of my free time there that summer, and in the fall enrolled at Columbia for courses in acting, direction and design. I worked with Milton Smith, who was a genius, and had a wonderful time.

Then, at a party, I met a new man. He was an actor and at an age and stage when he was thinking that he should be settled. One night after a bottle of Chianti – and much to his surprise, I think – he said we should get married. Even more to my surprise, I agreed. We moved to Australia, built a lovely house and eventually adopted two wonderful children. People assumed that I was a pro-

fessional actress and I did not correct them. I discovered that if one stays just five minutes ahead of the pack and says, 'Yes – I can do that,' almost anything is possible.

I told no one that every job – every new challenge – was a 'first' and prayed that no questions would be asked! I acted on stage, on radio, on TV. Became one of 'the girls' on morning radio. A National Youth Theatre was proposed. I offered to lick stamps and raise funds. Three years later I was its executive director. It was a short jump from there to the State Theatre Company as director of programming, and a slightly longer leap to the Sydney Opera House to establish and manage its audience development programme. I had acquired – not so very suddenly – a high profile in the arts.

Somewhere along the line the marriage died. We had grown apart, had found different lives. I think that although he was proud of my success he resented my commitment. With hindsight the signs had been there for years.

Then I met someone who enchanted, challenged and inspired me. He encouraged me to study again and to formalise my management skills. So – at last – I went to university. But, apart from the legal strands, I hated the MBA course, which had seemed to be the obvious answer. 'So,' said my love, 'transfer to law – it will do you just as much good.' I was nearly forty-five. My children needed help with their homework at night so I got up at 4 a.m. to study. Eventually our son went to boarding school and our daughter to Brazil. I took the plunge, left my husband and the lovely house, and moved into a tiny terrace in the inner city, overlooking an arm of Sydney Harbour. And was free!

In 1982 I ordered a wig from London and a set of robes, and went to the Bar. I was the first woman to be admitted to my particular Chambers – and realised that I had a long row to hoe! I began to write – textbooks, scripts, poetry, reviews, law reports – to teach at the University of Technology and to speak – at conferences, meetings, conventions . . . ('Have mouth; will travel' might have been my watchword!) and took up competitive sailing.

Seven years later, the opportunity came to join an international law firm to look at intellectual property in new technologies. I opted for that. At fifty-seven I moved to Singapore to establish an Asian telecommunications practice for a new firm. Two years later there was a merger and a new managing partner. 'Telecoms', he said, 'is a young man's game.' The office was closed and I was out in the cold, 'retired'. I was sixty.

How did it feel to be sixty? I felt no different from when I was thirty – and much better than I had at twenty. But for the first and only time in my life I felt discriminated against. Alone. Disempowered. And without a discernible future.

That Christmas I went to Bali and Jogjakarta. Then, in the new year, to Botswana and Zimbabwe, followed by trekking in North Thailand. Having blued the savings, I went home. And walked the dog. I visited old friends (thank God for good friends – they are a bulwark against self-pity), watched the remaining capital dwindle and waited for something to happen. Little did.

Eventually, light dawned. I had no pension (the money had all gone on educating the children and keeping the wolf from the door after the divorce, then, later, on French hats and champagne!) but the house was mortgage free and the young well launched in their careers. I had management and legal skills, intellectual and analytical capacity, as well as experience in dealing with budgets, government departments, personnel and public relations. So far in my life everything had just 'happened'. I had never even had to ask for a job. Now I had to take control!

A colleague asked me to join him in founding a boutique international legal firm in Singapore, with offices there and in Sydney. I commuted the eight hours regularly, but as I never suffered from jet lag, this was no chore. Elected to the board in three international telecommunications organisations, I travelled the world on their business. My daughter and I rediscovered a close relationship and friendship and, after my mother came to live in Australia following my father's death, we eventually diminished the distance between us. Most importantly, I realised that no one else could be made responsible for my happiness. The isolation of my childhood had given me the capacity to be content in my own company and I had been privileged to enjoy four careers, any one of which I would have paid good money to experience.

What did sixty feel like? Absolutely fabulous!

Four years later I packed everything I valued into a container and returned to England. My professional partner, sadly, had died. I was ready for a new adventure and a different horizon. I had long wanted to live in the country and to make a cottage garden. So I bought a fifteenth-century farmhouse in Suffolk, and when I was not working or travelling, began to dig. A herb garden – herbaceous borders – a new orchard – a potager – and a big pond for the ducks and geese. Hens now roam freely and doves wheel between the dovecotes, unperturbed by the prowlings of the two resident mouse controllers.

I am often asked what possible connection there can be between these different lives – how could nursing connect to the theatre; the theatre to the law? There has been a progression – layers of experience bonded together over time. The raw lives of my factory friends prepared me for many of the people I nursed. They in turn provided rich inspiration for performance and writing. Ward management was not so different from managing a company of actors and the skills developed in the theatre were invaluable when teaching or addressing a jury. I hope that the conglomeration of experience has enabled me better to understand my children, my godchildren and my grandchild. I find them all enchanting.

Our mothers and grandmothers were generally denied this kind of diversity and were, by the time they reached sixty, firmly settled into early old age, while I, and many of my contemporaries, are still considering the options for our next careers!

GILLIAN RECKITT

Just one more career!

When you are compulsorily retired from your job at sixty, it might be tempting to take it easy; but that would never have suited Gillian Reckitt.

Here I am, sixty-four years of age, running a Whitstable café with my daughter Josephine and just starting the third year of our venture together – and please don't let me ever suffer those first two years again! Josephine is a chef, I am a good administrator, but we have *never* done anything like this before. But then my life has always been full of surprises and new careers.

In the 1950s, when I left school, 'Higher Education' wasn't really an option. University places were as scarce as a hen's teeth and, not being blessed with an academic brain, the obvious opening for me was to be 'secretarial'. Shorthand at 120 wpm and bookkeeping, plus fast and accurate typing took me into the business world in London, then to Yorkshire where I became PA to my uncle, who ran the family brewery, then off to Canada for two years where I was ribbed mercilessly by my French Canadian boss who was always asking me to 'take a French letter please, Gillian'!

At twenty-three years of age I took my first 'plane ride – a long one, to Singapore. Again employed as a secretary, this time in the Foreign Office, life became a whirl of dances, cocktail parties, beach picnics, water-skiing and sailing – with the occasional bit of work fitted in. I was fortunate enough to be taken round the world by my boss, which incurred the wrath and envy of my fellow FO employees.

After a year in Singapore I was 'promoted' to become PA to the British Consul in Taiwan – a dubious honour as Taiwan didn't have diplomatic relations with Britain, so we Brits led a pretty lonely life, not very often being seen in public, in case Chiang Kai-shek or Madame Chiang encountered us. Being on the other side of the world gave me an opportunity to visit my father's family – descendants of the Bounty – now residing on Norfolk Island, a tiny spot in the South Pacific. This was the beginning of a love story with the island, where I now have a small home and had intended to spend six months of every year.

In 1962, at the ripe old age of twenty-five, I returned to the UK, worked for a smart American oil company in Berkeley Square, London, met my husband-to-be and married. All within six months. The next four years brought two daughters, Helena, now working in Atlanta, Georgia, and Josephine.

At the end of the Sixties various coincidences took me, via part-time employment in an employment agency, into my own agency focusing on the advertising business. The business thrived over the years, until in the Eighties I had five small companies and over 400 temporary members of staff working for my partners and me.

I decided to go it alone in life at the age of fifty-two and retired at fifty-five, having only just survived the ghastly British recession. I planned to spend two years scuba diving round the world, as one does at fifty-five! It was less than a year later, in Australia and planning to start a small business there, that my younger daughter was taken ill in England and I had to come home without delay. I had let my house there and finances were fairly strained.

So back to work I went, just as a temporary clerk/typist, terrified of all the new technology that awaited me. Most of the young secretaries were helpful and charming, but one remarked that since I was a trained secretary she could not understand why I didn't know how to work the printer and had a constant battle with the fax machine. She was astounded when I explained to her about manual typewriters, carbon paper, Tipp-Ex, the complete lack of copying machines except for those roneo machines – with wax sheets and lots of very messy ink. She was more helpful after that.

That part-time job turned eventually into an offer to take over the boss's role, and from there I was headhunted to managing the graduate trainees of the company, and I spent four very happy years with a great group of young people, who didn't seem to mind being nannied by an almost-sixty-year-old! But all good things come to an end, and I was a victim of compulsory retirement at sixty. On to better things, thought I. No money in it, but lots of new friends and new places. I worked at Buckingham Palace during the summer season after I retired, and became the chief loo cleaner – nobody else seemed to want this chore, but I found it most rewarding – meeting and greeting ladies from all parts of the world.

After that, retired, I spent many months on Norfolk Island each year, struggling a bit financially, with one house in London and another on Norfolk Island, and a rather expensive journey between the two. I had never thought my life would take such a turn.

My younger daughter, now fully recovered from her long illness, had moved to Whitstable in Kent and was working in Canterbury as a chef. She had been cordon bleu trained in London and had worked as a chef in lots of restaurants, including a spell in Melbourne, Australia. I had been summoned to 'dog sit' while she and a group of friends did a big catering job at the Eclipse Festival at the Lizard in Cornwall. Whitstable was, as I already knew, charming, rather 'olde worlde' and still not far from London, where I had my house.

I was walking the dog on the beach, sun shining, everything right with the world when *wham* – 'Why not move here?' I thought. It would solve all my financial problems. I could pay off the mortgage on the house on Norfolk Island with the sale of the house in London and have a good quarter of a million left over to buy a place in Whitstable.

Most of the house agents just didn't want to know – a house with a sea frontage . . . somewhere you can park . . . you haven't sold your house in London yet . . . and many other discouraging comments. Until I came to see Shirley – certainly the best, most efficient and kindest estate agent I have ever met. Not only have we remained friends, but her son has also spent a year working for us in the café. Shirley announced that she had taken details of the most perfect house for me *that day* and she knew that my house in London would sell within four weeks.

My daughter arrived back from Cornwall at dawn the following morning, was quickly marched round to see the house, which was simply perfect, and we went back to the agency to put in an offer, which was subsequently accepted. Just looking around the agency we noticed that a local café was for sale . . .

In my day we would have called the Harbour Street Café a bistro – but that isn't cool, so it is a café. We specialise in organic, free-range, vegetarian, vegan, gluten-free and unusual food. Not unusual for London, perhaps, but for Whitstable, where you can eat fish, fish or fish, our food is going down a storm. Have a look at our website www.harbourstreetcafe.co.uk . . .

But hard work is an understatement – Josephine is major domo of the kitchen and the food, but the staff management, bookkeeping (all on the computer – yikes!), wages, laundry, etc. are mostly down to me. At the beginning a fourteen-hour day was a short one, but now, into our second year, life is getting easier.

We aren't making any money yet, but at least we haven't gone under, which is what I believe happens to a large number of small companies in their first year. My accountant tells me that we shouldn't make a profit yet and that seems an easy order. Perhaps in three years there might be enough to pay me a wage, even possibly some rent for my investment. But fortunately, life in Whitstable is a lot easier and cheaper than in London and my travelling certainly has been curbed, particularly since I am now a granny, thanks to my head chef, Josephine.

Who knows what I will be doing by the time I am seventy! – yet another new career, perhaps?

JANE FREEBAIRN-SMITH

The golden thread

It has to be exciting to be where you really want to be in your life, even if it took until your sixties to get there. Jane Freebairn-Smith, now a priest, describes her journey.

I am now, in my sixties, a parish priest in the diocese of Lincoln. God has been important all through my life. God has given meaning and purpose to me even though my images of and relationship with Him have changed and I have known periods of doubt.

This sense of continuity has been like a golden thread running through a life with its many changes, deaths and resurrections. I was adopted at birth and although I have tried to trace them I have never discovered my birth family. This has raised the question 'who am I?' as I know nothing of my roots. It is wonderfully liberating to know who I am in my sixties and that I am now part of two families, my children and my parish. There will, however, always be a sense of the unknown about my past as well as, of course, the future. Faith and hope therefore become even more important.

I was ordained a priest in St Mary's Cathedral, Glasgow in December 1994. I was fifty-nine years old. There were seven of us at this first ordination of women. I felt as if I was part of history in the making – a pioneer. As I look back, my life had prepared me for this moment. It was immensely moving and awe-inspiring, the ordination among people I have known and loved, some of whom have travelled with me in my pilgrimage over many years. Two of them were priests who had both had a major part in my spiritual development and vocation. One of them had prepared me for confirmation in 1951, had never come to terms with women's ordination and yet was supportive even until his death in 1989. The other, whom I have known for many years, was one of the priests who shared in the laying on of hands.

The next day when I celebrated the Eucharist in the Cathedral I felt a great sense of privilege, especially as I gave the bread to each person – at one with them in prayer, knowing their joys and sorrows.

I was brought up in the Church of England from birth. My paternal grandfather was a priest, both as a missionary in Africa and here in England. My parents went to church every Sunday. One story from my very early childhood was being taken to church on a toboggan. Another early memory was wondering why we said in church each Sunday 'I believe in . . . the holy Catholic Church'. I went to a Roman Catholic convent school but I knew I was C of E.

At a conference not long after school I discovered that the Church of England did train and license women as parish workers or deaconesses. The first seeds of vocation were sown then. Soon I realised I did not want at that time to be a deaconess, dressed up and sitting in the choir. I wanted to sit with the laity in the pews and to identify with them. The church did not seem to value her greatest resource, her people and their potential for ministry. In January 1961 I became a parish worker in the Canterbury diocese with this strong sense of vocation to empower lay people, a thread that has run through the whole of my developing vocation and ministry.

At the time, I was content to be a parish worker. I did not think that women should be priests. Some people in the parish did, however, comment that I was the kind of woman they would like to see as a priest. That sowed new seeds in my mind.

The second stage of the journey came twenty years later, by which time I was married with three very special children, two daughters and a son, and was living in Scotland. I loved being a mother and a homemaker. I never regretted being at home full time with them although there were few spare pennies. They were precious years in which I could be with the family and watch them grow up. They are all now grown-up, working, married and with their own children. I became a grandmother in 1999 to a grand-daughter and two grandsons within seven weeks of each other. They are, of course, a joy and delight.

It was in 1981, when the children were well into their teens, that I became more involved with the Scottish Episcopal Church serving on many of its provincial and diocesan boards and committees. I still felt like a parish worker but as I watched the legislation develop that would create women deacons, a new way of responding to God's call began to stir. I wrestled with the idea at the time as I still felt that it was important to have lay people in active ministry. But Holman Hunt's picture of *Christ the Light of the World* above the altar, which I looked at each week, spoke to me. I could see Christ knocking at the door and I knew that the handle lay on the other side and only I could open it. I was made a deacon in 1988 and ordained priest in 1994.

Looking back, there have been so many experiences which seem to have prepared me for this stage of life. There was, to start with, a childhood with many upheavals and changes. For the first three years we lived in Surrey. Then the war came and the whole family was moved to Scotland through my father's work. My mother suffered a depression within a year and I was taken south to stay briefly with my mother's sister and then for the rest of the time with my father's spinster sister. I had started school in Scotland so I moved school as well, this time to a convent school in

Surrey as a day girl. After the war we were reunited, which had its own difficulties. My mother and aunt did not get on, and we took a year to get our house back. We lived for some months in the International Language Club in Croydon in one room.

Finally, we returned home and I went to a private school, until I passed the 11-plus and went to the local grammar school. I was there two terms when my father retired (he was much older than my mother) and we moved to Kent and I changed school again. Towards the end of my teens my mother had another period of depression and I went to stay with our vicar and his wife. It was through them that I at last began to learn what it meant to be a parent. I stayed with them until I had my own flat when I became a parish worker.

After all these changes and disruptions I wanted so much to settle and to have a sense of belonging. I found much of that belonging through marriage and my own children but also through the family of the church. I then discovered, to my surprise, that my upbringing, as I listened to other people's stories, was quite privileged by comparison, yet it was sheltered from the world outside and I was very naive when I married. I did have a midlife crisis, during which I trained as a counsellor. That helped me to become more self-aware, confident and, I hope, more compassionate and understanding.

The sense of sadness and failure that my marriage was never happy came to an end in 1995 when we separated and I moved to my present parish. We are now divorced. I discovered that I was able to find a greater integrity, the freedom to be myself and a personal fulfilment as a priest, even at the age of fifty-nine.

And what of the joys and sorrows of being a parish priest. Every day is different as I respond to the needs of the people in this place and exercise a role of leadership: the privilege of being with the bereaved and making the funeral service right for them; baptising babies including my own grandchildren; marrying people and sharing in their joy, especially if one or both of them have been divorced and found happiness again; dealing with the unexpected; watching the water in the font disappear before I had hardly baptised the first of two babies – it was a country church with no hall or running water – being presented with a dirty nappy by a wedding guest after a wedding – it is useful to carry a 'poly' bag in my cassock pocket! – being told by a bride the looped petticoat was slipping in the middle of the service.

I am enjoying being a priest who is also myself. It is immensely rewarding and fulfilling. At times it can be frustrating and sad when you see someone unhappy or stuck, or worried through illness or because of family difficulties. But above all it is a privilege to share other people's lives at a deep level and walk with them on their spiritual journey. I wouldn't change it for anything.

Strength from tears

Trials and tribulations can make or mar us.
Joan Robinson describes how she dealt with a
succession of them as she approached
her sixties.

The year 2000 ended with lots of celebrations. I had survived the traumas of divorce, a brain operation, two strokes, a broken jaw and the realisation that I would always be financially insecure because of my depleted circumstances. Yet I could rejoice. I was alive! God had spared me. I really do believe that each of us has a guardian angel and that we are here for a purpose.

Because of what I went through I can now honestly say that I am stronger, more understanding of other people's needs, more positive than I was before, and with a deep spiritual belief that my soul is truly my own. What I need I have, anything I want I can do without.

On my sixtieth birthday I looked at myself in the mirror and I liked the person who was staring back. So! This is an image of sixty, at best I can now look forward to another twenty or so years. Good!

I come from Jamaica. Both my parents were born on the island, met and got married there. They died within six months of each other, both in their eighties. I had my formative schooling up to high school standard in Jamaica and came to the UK with my mother in the mid-Fifties. I was placed in a south London girls' high school and from there went into further education at a college in south London where I gained favourable results in my exams. What were my ambitions? I didn't have a clue.

I had met a young man while still in college but was advised by my parents to finish my studies before even thinking of forming a relationship which could jeopardise any academic ambitions I might be harbouring. Looming before me was the choice of continuing with my studies or getting married to this man I was head over heels in love with. I chose the latter.

Before I could figure out what life was all about I had three children under five years old at home, a husband to look after and a home to manage. My husband's job meant the family travelling around the UK as well as overseas. I had to prove that I was quite capable of travelling and managing home and family with the minimum of fuss. This would eventually take its toll on my health. Good housekeeping? There is another name for it: stress development.

A plan of action was needed. The children were growing up and doing very well in their studies. I began to organise what spare time I could afford to develop my existing skills and learn new ones when the opportunity presented itself. I registered at a nearby college and did a series of business and finance courses. When that was over I entered the world of paid employment on a full-time basis. In no time at all I was in middle management. The feel good factor couldn't have been more in evidence. But D-Day was approaching.

It is now the late 1980s. My husband was working in America with a view to our maybe moving over there on our retirement. It was May Bank Holiday, sunny, warm, late spring going into summer. The phone rang. My husband was calling to ask me to pick him up from the bus stop across from our street. The butter-

flies began to flutter in my stomach. I knew instinctively something was wrong.

My husband had met someone in the USA who was twenty or more years younger than himself, had had an affair and come back to the UK to get himself sorted out emotionally.

My whole life came to a standstill. Other people got divorced, not us. This came at a time when everything seemed to be going so well. Good jobs, a Mercedes Benz, a house, savings in the bank. My husband's prospects were good and we were working towards a comfortable retirement. I thought, 'Who altered the script?' Devoted wives and mothers do not get treated like this. No way!

The downward spiral began. I collapsed at work in 1992 and had a brain operation in 1993, which rendered me incapable of doing the type of management work I was trained for. I began to feel like a trapped animal. I was fighting with my speech, my balance, eyesight, not to mention the excess weight I had put on due to medication and inactivity. I went from size 14 to 18 in no time at all. When I came home from the hospital I could not walk up the stairs. I had to go up on my buttocks backwards and down on my buttocks holding on to the rail. I was struggling to keep my balance, my short-term memory was useless, depression was setting in. I was sliding down into a dark place and could do nothing to help it.

After five years of separation my husband got his divorce in 1994, but he had not settled with me re property etc. It was about this time that I joined the organisation Fair Shares, lobbying the government for pensions on divorce. I realised that my husband had walked away with his civil service pension and had not shared it with me after thirty-plus years of marriage. I felt I had to contribute to the organisation's effort to fight for a better deal for divorced women. It was to be too late for me but others would benefit. Eventually, on 9 June 1998, the headlines in the papers read: DIVORCED WIVES WIN A SHARE OF PENSIONS. Meantime I was also giving more time to my other voluntary organisations. In 1995, almost two years after the brain operation, I was acting as the PR person for Black Women's Promotion when I received an invitation to attend the fourth World Women's Conference as a delegate at the United Nations Headquarters in New York.

At the end of the first day of that conference I came out of the main entrance of the UN building. I looked across at Roosevelt Boulevard and the Hudson river, placed my briefcase on the ground, threw up my hands and punched the air with a loud exclamation of 'Yes!'. My wings were firmly in place. The tears streamed down my face, I was shaking a bit.

My speech was still a little slurred, my balance not good but I was holding my own. Here on my own merit, interacting with like-minded men and women who wanted to make a difference by defending human rights, arguing the cases of those who could not do it for themselves. I was invited on to radio programmes, to the Women Writers' Guild of New York. I ran workshops on behalf of the BWP. Then, back in London in 1996, I was invited to the Woman of the Year lunch at the Savoy. I felt like a bird. I could fly!

1997 saw me back in New York by kind invitation of the New York State University. The highlight was the million women march in Philadelphia. The march was about determined women of all shades, sizes and backgrounds, women beating a spiritual drum that told them anything is possible.

In 1998 I suffered a stroke. Time stood still for a short period. I would be talking on the phone and as soon as the conversation came to an end, so did the memory of whom I was speaking to. The slurring started again. My taste buds were affected. Sometimes I could not tell if the food was on my face or in my mouth. At one stage I nearly asked my daughter to go out and buy me some paddy pads. The very thought of being fifty-something years old and having to resort to that filled me with horror and despair.

In 1999 I had another stroke. This time my left side was affected. When I came out of hospital I had to work even harder at recovering. My left leg felt as though it had two house bricks tied to it. I was not in control and the frustration was building up. Simple things like making a cup of tea or getting biscuits from a tin were a performance. Then I thought of all those people in wheelchairs, those who were bedridden, war victims, men, women and children who were having to manage without their limbs. I would say a prayer and thank God for his mercies. I was on the mend. I could feel better days were coming, and they have.

I thank my children for being such warm and loving human beings whose support I could not have done without. I thank my friends who were there for me and those who created an opportunity for me to be heard. I will also thank my ex-husband. I was ill, unemployable, scared out of my wits. I thank him for letting it be proven once again that women are strong-minded and do not have to be victims if we do not want to be. Let yesterday's tears become the seeds of today's hope, renewal and strength.

JOANNA FOSTER

Repairing the patchwork

*How do you rebuild your life in your sixties
when your husband of forty years unexpectedly
leaves you for another? Joanna Foster
describes how it feels.*

Elizabeth took this photo the day after my mother died – the day the sun was in total eclipse. One year later my son got married and my husband left me for someone else. What a long time ago it now seems – another life. The photograph captures me sitting under the very fruitful old vine in the conservatory of Confessor's Gate – my home. In front of me is my laptop.

As I look at the photo now I see it as a symbol of what the last eighteen months have been. The laptop is a sharp reminder that unless I press the keys in a certain logical order I will find it very difficult to make progress. The problem has been that logic has not played a very useful role in helping me come to terms with my new life. Nor has it helped me get down to writing this piece. My head has frequently told me that it is time to put all the shocks and horrors behind me and to start rebuilding my life. My heart has lagged painfully behind. Procrastination and uncertainty about the past, present or future have been corrupting my promises to get writing.

It is now the beginning of a new year. Time again to prune the conservatory vine, keeping the strong branches and cutting out the meandering, straggly ones. Time to make a huge bonfire and time to move on. The challenge is how much to prune back and how much to burn.

I was the product of a girls' boarding school and the parental expectation that my two brothers would go to university, which they did, and that I would do a secretarial course. I went on to work on magazines, newspapers and with prime ministers; I founded a language school and worked in an international business school with managers and their families in Fontainebleau, France and at the University of Pittsburgh in the USA. Later, back in the UK, I led the campaign for developing young people at work as well as the equal opportunities and women's development work at the Industrial Society in London. Being president of Relate and chairing the Equal Opportunities Commission, the International Year of the Family, the BT Forum and the National Work Life Forum gave me a national profile. But that was the past.

For most of my life I have considered that I have been one of the happiest, luckiest women I know. I have had a series of incredibly interesting and fulfilling jobs working with people who have inspired and encouraged me. I have made many friends and, most precious of all, I have been surrounded and supported by my extraordinary family, in particular my husband. On what would have been our fortieth wedding anniversary my thoughts inevitably drifted back to the past. I was taking part in a two-day Shakespeare workshop; it was wonderfully enjoyable and distracting. The fields surrounding the house were full of white daisies.

They reminded me of the graveyard at the church where we were married.

We met in France when I was seventeen. We were married just after my twenty-second birthday. The church is where my parents are now buried and our first child was baptised after months of going through the whole drawn-out and highly emotional time leading up to the adoption process. Then came golden years with two children, living in France and the States before returning to Oxford. Friends, family, lots of laughter and lots of work.

Then the sun slowly started its eclipse. Things began to change. Five bonus years of sharing our house and his death with my nonagenarian father-in-law were followed by my mother's death. I was sad – but free. No more anxious worries about carers, no more colourful and frequently told stories about Victorian childhood. An end to trying to explain why I was no more neglecting my children when I was not there at teatime than she had by sending me to boarding school.

It was a strange transition time as we became the older generation. It was also a liberating time, as I contemplated how the patchwork of my life might change. There was the prospect of fewer obligations and less but still interesting work – both paid and gifted; of the children building their own lives; of more time for us as a couple, for fun with friends, for travelling and for those interesting conversations about the meaning of life. Instead – while eating lunch at the kitchen table – my husband announced that he was off to find the meaning of life with someone else.

I have spent the last eighteen months crying more than I thought was physically possible. I have yearned for my old golden life but I have also wondered whether I had imagined it all. Could I trust my memories? The pain of losing so much in so short a time has been acute. My children, my daughter-in-law, my brothers and their wives and children have been extraordinary. My friends too: thoughtful Sunday evening calls, patient listening, many hankies, bottles of wine and encouragement as I have tried to pick up my life again.

Work keeps me busy. I currently chair the Lloyds TSB Foundation and the Nuffield Orthopaedic Centre, NHS Trust in Oxford. I am also deputy chair of Oxford Brookes University and a visiting professor at Bristol University. I continue in my work to speak at lots of conferences and to many different groups of people. I also work with individual women and men as a coach and I have found that the training to become a coach, combined with a leadership course at the Harvard Business School, has ignited my desire to get back to study. I have always integrated my own life experience into my work. I have also always tried to live out my strongly held personal values about trying to reconcile my professional life with my family and community life. This has been a driving force for me over the years and has been at the heart of so much of my campaigning work.

I learn from other people's experience and I believe that other people find it quite helpful to do the same thing. So, for the first time this week, I have talked in public about being left. I have talked about the effect this has had on my self-esteem, about the way it has sapped my personal and professional confidence and my creative energy. I have described how dire it has been to lose my sense of humour, my ability to make decisions, or to be able accurately to remember the past or envisage a future. I have even been able to express the huge longing I have had to have my old life back and again to be one of a couple.

You will know when things are getting better, good friends have constantly told me. I know now and they are. It has been a long, staged journey with many circular diversions and blind alleys. I have learned that living by myself can be enjoyable; that having my children and friends to talk with, play with, eat with and cry with is beyond price; that driving around Europe alone can be fun; that sorting out bills, wilful computers and broken boilers is not; that a good therapist is my lifeline along with e-mail, the telephone and my garden.

Embarking on a new life at sixty-two is just beginning to seem exciting.

Six months after writing this I received a CBE in the Queen's Jubilee Honours for services to the world of work and equal opportunities. A lovely surprise, and the huge numbers of enthusiastic letters, calls and e-mails from friends and colleagues, past and present, have been wonderful.

KATHRYN KIRKLAND-HANDLEY

The call of Hecate

Life is mysterious. In response to grief and sadness we can sometimes unlock hidden parts of ourselves. Kathryn Kirkland-Handley describes what happened to her.

In January 2001 I marked my sixty-fourth year of life. 'Aha!' I thought, 'now I am a crone.' I liked the sound of that word, 'crone'. Strangely, with the recognition of this last stage of life, I began to feel younger and younger with each passing month. Not physically, it was a feeling that sprang from inner certitude.

My life has changed over and over again in so many unexpected ways. Somehow I have survived all the tides of time. My burgeoning inner life is the result of continual yielding to the unexpected. I look back to see how my life flowed from childhood into maidenhood, from offering service and self-sacrifice in motherhood into a deepening authenticity and emerging wisdom as a crone.

My story is a litany of death and renewal. At each juncture of my life, whether consciously chosen or not, an ending or a death has preceded each birth, every beginning. I have had to give up something profoundly important to me, someone deeply loved, to make space for unexpected enrichment to take place in my life.

In 1955 I left home for university with a desire to find a husband and an education – in that order. In 1963, having graduated, married and taught primary school, I moved to the east coast with my young husband, Dean, where I had a place at the Pennsylvania Academy of Fine Arts. I studied for only one year, for my heart was set on children. It was that ambition which initially honed my already determined character, for children did not come easily. Longing for babies, in 1963 and 1966 we adopted our two eldest daughters, Anne and Margaret. Two years later, in London, I gave birth for the first time, to our son, Glenn.

In France, in 1974, my second birth child, Alison, was born with a severe disability: athetoid cerebral palsy. It was her situation that spawned in me both a terrible anguish and the imperative to survive. It was her life, so physically compromised, that caused me to question the meaning of my own. Through Alison's struggles I slowly began to discover my own broken spirit and ignored gifts. These painful discoveries fertilised my latent potential. And, at the same time, my carefully constructed paradigm of the perfect bourgeois family cracked open.

Alison's many difficulties demanded full parental commitment to her needs. My anguish was that her bright mind was imprisoned in her body. Ali was never able to speak, to sit up, to hold a pencil, to move independently. Broken-hearted by her fate, for months after her diagnosis in Munich I considered both suicide and infanticide. I finally turned my back on such impulses and instead pledged to make her life as 'normal' as possible. Those long, joyful, painful eight years of Alison's life demanded huge sacrifices from each family member. Yet, by including Alison's different needs in our family rhythm, each member's sacrifice was doubly reimbursed. I felt the skies cried with us as we buried Alison's body in the Sheen Cemetery on a rainy day in May 1982.

Alison's death coincided with my elder three children's departure for university and boarding school. In one fell swoop I lost my identity in motherhood. Grieving my losses, I followed my husband around like a lost puppy until the hidden gem of my hitherto ignored creativity returned to my rescue. I prepared my portfolio at the Chelsea to gain a place at St Martin's School of Art. Thus the egg of authentic self-expression was laid. I warmed that egg as I graduated from St Martin's and trained in psychotherapy at the Psychosynthesis and Education Trust.

My first husband, Dean, and I had striven to keep our family healthy. Unable to grieve together, we separated just after my fifty-first birthday. Divorce followed three years later. The death of my marriage demanded more reflection. I sat on my egg of authenticity as I pondered the end of my bourgeois image of respectability. I asked myself, 'Who am I?' To find out I put on a backpack and went to India for two long periods of retreat.

The first three-month period in India included an organised walk to the Markha Valley in Ladakh. On that walk I met Nick who lived and worked as a clinical psychologist in the north of England, and we engaged in a courtship of seven years' duration, separated by 200 miles. In 1995 we married. My second retreat to India was one of silence for four months in Tamil Nadu at Shantivanam Ashram. The silence gave birth to a more profound and lasting spiritual search, which continues to be the pivotal point of my life today.

At sixty I retired from my London practice as a psychotherapist intending to devote three years to travel round the world with my husband, Nick. I had expected to return to my familiar Richmond home and my long-established London patterns. But when I moved out of one half of my home in Richmond to make space for tenants, some dark, under-part of myself realised that this leave-taking was final. Puzzled as I wept in each vacated room, I grieved for the place that had sheltered me for nineteen years. It seemed an extreme reaction to my practical intellect, but my body knew I was no longer rooted in England.

I did not travel the world; I only made it back to the land of my birth. Driving with Nick in our twenty-two foot recreation vehicle down the east coast of America, across the Deep South to Texas and New Mexico was a part of our plan. His heart was set on Santa Fe and the Four Corners. But when he returned to London for a break from the New World, I suddenly found myself independently purchasing a house in Abiquiu, New Mexico. This was not a reasoned choice. It seemed I simply stood inside a mad woman's body, someone who said, 'I'll have it, what's the price?' From that strange, inexplicable choice, a new life has been born, a new journey begun, in a direction determined by myself.

The egg I had warmed hatched. New Mexico, the southwestern state known for collecting misfits, is the place where the painter, Georgia O'Keeffe, lived and worked. She married the photographer, Alfred Stieglitz, and divided her time between New York City and Abiquiu. At the time of my impulsive purchase I did not know this, but it is useful to me today as I attempt to develop my new pattern of living between London and Abiquiu.

As I developed new skills in hand-built pottery and had a studio built, Nick and I went through the hell of a cross-cultural marriage. While he wrote his autobiography in the casita, I wrote poetry in my study. We attended marital counselling together. He could not understand what I was becoming. Neither could I. But

Hecate had appeared to me in dreams and I named our Abiquiu home 'Dark Moon' for her.

When Nick left New Mexico in the autumn of 2000 to set up his London practice, I stayed behind for four months. Alone in my bed, I listened to coyotes howl after the midnight hunt. I love the solitude and the thrill of meeting my own edge alone on a desert or forested path. I continue introspection. I look inside to find fierce goddess images reside in me – Hecate and Diana – who do not take a married woman's life seriously.

In December, as planned, I returned to London, to our Richmond home and to Nick. Slowly we are learning to respect each other's individuality and different needs as we live together and apart. New Mexico's raw landscape challenges my urban polish and makes me live on the edge. Nick's work as an existential psychotherapist in London fulfils his desire and allows him to follow his own spiritual path.

Thus, to the surprise of my more conventional side, I am striving to find a way into an increasingly unconventional life. Like Georgia O'Keeffe, I wish to divide my life into two parts: one in Abiquiu where I intend to concentrate on avenues of creativity and one in Richmond with my husband where I await the emergence of unforeseen opportunities. However, I state these plans with caution, for I have become respectful of Destiny. I acknowledge strong forces for change in and around me which are beyond my mere control.

Death and rebirth is my theme. I know life's passage is brief. Every moment counts. My goal is to live fully, with authenticity and decency. Experience has taught me that life flows inexorably in its own direction. My role as a fully fledged old bird, indeed a burgeoning crone, is to trust, conform to, even rejoice in that which arrives, for I now understand that however alone I may feel, I am not. I am surrounded and formed by Life's own determination to survive.

LEVANA MARSHALL

Four pillars and three poisons

What sustains us through life and into our sixties?
Levana Marshall, a psychotherapist, reflects on her
personal journey.

On the threshold of my sixtieth birthday I am no longer concerned with the questions of who I am, what I have achieved
in life and what the meaning of life might be.

These big issues seem irrelevant and misguiding at this stage
in my life. I am here, I have arrived, and I am full of wonder and
awe as to how it all happened, how I've been living an unfolding
story, a story created by the intimate interaction of my own personal inner forces, and, more interestingly, external life forces.
How much did I personally will things to happen and how much
did I have to yield to unforeseen winds?

My maternal grandmother was called Sol (in Spanish – sun).
My paternal grandmother was called Luna (in Spanish – moon).

She was a matriarch – wise and sharp-minded with a compassion-ate sense of humour. I was named after her, Levana being the Hebrew for moon. My family came from Greece, of Jewish-Span-ish descent. My Israeli-Jewish heritage is the first pillar that would enrich and sustain my being.

At the age of twenty-one I got married to Morris, an Indian Jew who is my soul and body mate. We left Israel hungry and curi-ous to discover the world. The world was fascinating – the Far East, Europe. Our son Oren was born in Geneva, our daughter Shanit in Hong Kong. We did not conquer the world, it conquered us. Exposure to different cultures, languages and people was a second pillar that would teach me diverse ways of thinking and living.

With two children who needed stability and consistency, we settled in England, the home of psychoanalysis. My Israeli-Jewish boundaries received many blows. The pain of transformation was biting and trying. Who was I becoming? A stranger to my country and a foreigner in the world? What was my place? I had to seek the answer within myself through psychoanalysis. This became my third pillar of strength and wisdom, a mode of enquiry and explo-ration into the self.

In my twenties I learned to become a wife and a mother. In my thirties I learned about psychic pain and trained as a psychol-ogist and psychotherapist. I acquired tools to practise awareness and to find ways to access the recesses of my mind, linking present patterns of behaviour and interaction with life to childhood expe-riences. Psychoanalysis stripped from me the delusion that I was omnipotent enough to live the perfect life – the life created in my mind. I had to accept my deep connection to my parents, and to my culture, and to learn to accept my wounded being.

In my forties I was fascinated by the larger systems and struc-tures that shaped me. I trained as a family therapist and a group analyst. I was, for five years, in a twice-weekly group, exposed to

the forces that shift and manifest themselves in a group as a whole, to the fact that each member expresses an aspect of the group's life. How does it happen? If I am a manifestation of a particular thought or emotion that is latent in the group, then who precisely am I?

Today I can say with great relief that I do not exist without the other. I am a participant and a witness to life. Like a shaman. We are all each other's servant. I'm saying this with the sense of appreciation of the beauty of it. We try so hard to deny this reality and defend ourselves by trying to be the masters of each other. I realised in my forties that my quest has been like a sculptor facing a block of stone, chipping away from myself in order to become more myself. I seek to dissolve through my husband, my children, my friends, and into them. I dissolve and change continuously, but I am also steely and unshakeable.

I have always been passionate about finding and exploring the paradoxes in which I live. This exploration led me to seek a spiritual master in my fifties. For the last nine years I have travelled the world, following the greatest masters of Buddhist teachings – Tibetan Buddhism, and Zen. My fourth pillar of wisdom, the teachings of the Buddha, touched me directly. Life is suffering – we are born, grow old, become ill and die. Through psychotherapy I trained myself to accept it, deal with it and cope the best I could. What was new and different was the push to free myself from this suffering. It did not mean that I would be free from pain, from the day-to-day struggle and anguish. It meant a change in my whole relationship with life, treating life as an intimate friend who teaches us to find the way to our true nature beyond life and death.

The work is hard and relentless. To be free in life and death I have to be free from the three main poisons – anger, attachment and ignorance – poisons that contaminate us all. My own personal difficulty, and I think I am right in saying that it is true of most humans, is that we believe the statements that our minds tell us. We are attached to our feelings, thoughts and ideas, and we confuse them with who we are. We are trapped with our 'programme'.

In the last three years I've lost a few beloved friends, and my father. I challenge myself to prepare to die. I cannot control how, when and the way it will happen. What I can do is observe my mind bringing up the debris of a lifetime, seducing me to believe that my fears are expressions of truth.

I want to be able to get to the end of my journey knowing the face I had before my parents were born. I want to be able to smile with compassion to myself on my deathbed (if there's going to be a bed). To smile at the messes I created in my life, the terrible destructions I was involved in, the beautiful garden I created, the deep, deep love I have for Morris, for my children, for life – and for death.

MEREDITH HOOPER

Me and me

Family or Antarctica – or both? How can one combine responsibilities for family life with the chance to spend Antarctic summers as writer in residence with American and Australian researchers? Meredith Hooper describes the dilemma and how the experience changed her.

I've always written, ever since I was a child. But when I began writing books I fitted them in, between my primary obligations – pencil and paper on the car seat at traffic lights on the school run to scribble the sentences I was in the middle of when the clock said, 'leave now'. Grabbing a moment on the way from the shower at the start of the day, catching the ideas which had come in the night. Publishers' advances paid for au pairs to carve me the time. But everything else came first. My husband and his work, the children and their needs, running the house and the garden. That was the given.

There's nothing strange or unfamiliar about this. It was the way we were brought up. The assumptions welded deep in our

137

beings. Girls were, as they always had been, for marrying, ideally by twenty-one, certainly not too much later. When I fell in love I wrote in my diary, with not a hint of irony, or question, 'Farewell career.' That was the attitude of almost everyone around me – contemporaries, as much as the older generation of potential advisers. I was at Oxford on a postgraduate scholarship from Australia, one of a small group who had been selected to continue studying 'overseas'. I'd begun an academic career. But that's what happened to girls. They fell in love, they got married. Careers petered out. I was innately passive and I accepted it without question.

So I wrote my books, mostly non-fiction, mainly for children, with the passion I'd given to my academic research. The books fitted the timescales I could create. I kept my papers in cardboard boxes, migrating from tables to desks wherever there was a temporary space. I didn't give myself permission to spend money on infrastructure. I used second-hand files, the backs of used paper, old envelopes. No one told me I had to.

Looking back, it seems bizarre. But thinking about it now, I had no real belief in my right to be carving out this time for myself ahead of other priorities. The realities of family and home commitments didn't make allowances. As long as they came first (to quote my upbringing). Which, of course, they did; which I didn't question.

So far, so conventional.

I achieved a body of publications and made minor moves back in to the edges of academe. I did it, like a number of my contemporaries, by negotiating gaps, buying opportunities, forcing the hours, stealing time. I knew a few women who successfully combined full careers with high-achieving husbands and responsibility for children, and admired them as super-endowed with energy. I failed on the energy stakes. For me, family life was hard, fulfilling work. But I was really happy. My writing came second. If it didn't fit in, I didn't do it.

Then came the unconventional. I removed myself physi-cally. I didn't plan it, or seek it out. It happened. Extracting from multi-layered responsibilities, the totality of relationships. Unhooking the anchors. No longer available as the family's resource. Going away, on my own. Not for the weekend, or a week. But two and a half months. To the other end of the world. I was unobtainable. Ungettable.

And it was absolute, magical bliss. It was freedom.

My youngest son had just started university. 'My mother', he would tell his friends mournfully, 'thinks that penguins are more important than her family.'

At fifty-five, I was on an ice-breaker heaving through mon-strous seas heading south, south, as far as you could go. I had been selected by the Australian National Antarctic Research Expedi-tions to travel to Antarctica as a writer.

I was on my own again. And I reached out, and found me – the original, before-marriage-at-twenty-four me. I didn't know I was still here. I didn't know the original me was waiting, or that I hadn't been that me, in between. I'd been so caught up in my new life. But there I still was. The person who didn't belong to anyone else, who didn't need to put all the people I loved first. Suddenly, miraculously, I had the right to put myself first. I could make the decisions about what to do, and when. So of course me and me worked together with total contentment. We only had ourselves to consider. I decided what to do without having to think about those who depended on me, because no one did. I talked to whom I pleased. I got up when I woke up and went to bed when I was ready. I worked exactly the hours I wanted, when I wanted. Being precipitated into a world where my work had intrinsic status and value was heady.

Three times in Antarctica I was able to ring home. And I could send a few faxes. That was it and I didn't mind one bit. The time was so precious, and clear. I had no desire to fill it with the all-

important everyday events of other people's lives. No point clut-
tering it emotionally. Of course I love my family. But I didn't fret,
or pine.

I got a huge amount of writing done. Twice what I'd planned.
All meals and accommodation provided. The time mine – life was
an unexpected re-creation of my Oxford college. Antarctica was
intellectually stretching, physically challenging. I discovered I was
braver than I'd ever thought. More physically able. I achieved
things I'd never imagined even tackling. I'm not athletic, or
strong, but I did things because they were there to do – I pushed
my limits out.

And I came back changed. For ever.

Fitting back into the role waiting for me, like pushing a tree back into its hole, wasn't easy. It was difficult for me, because I'd changed, and hadn't expected it. Difficult for my family because they didn't know I had changed and naturally didn't want it, nor the implications. They were happy with the existing model.

One implication of the change was a second trip south. This time I went for three and a half months. Of course your husband is going with you, people said. Firmly. Slightly accusingly. Did I accompany him on his many business trips away, over the years? No. But this wasn't even a business trip. I'd been awarded a place on the American Antarctic Artists & Writers Program, run by the National Science Foundation. I'd gone through a long application process. Berths and beds in Antarctica are scarce and competitive. The grant wasn't for partners. But that was difficult for many friends and acquaintances to grasp. Because basically, to them, I was abandoning my husband.

So once again I went south, to live and work as me, for a quarter of the year. This time e-mail had been inserted into Antarctic life, breaching remoteness with its instant cross-world access. Part of the critical magic of Antarctica for me had been its inaccessibility. I could allocate my resources to my work. Physical removal meant freedom. Now, with e-mail, the body might be gone, but the mind was available. The outside world could plug into my attention. I had to work harder to replace eroded time.

But I've just gone again. The National Science Foundation selected me to return to the ice. My family now accept my decision. They do support it. Friends still tend to be puzzled.

Antarctica has become my research base. It's one of the places I work. It's also, I admit, with a kind of nineteenth-century recognition, an addiction. I'm addicted to this extraordinary continent.

And, I've finally learned, I have the right to do it.

It's a small change. To my daughter and her contemporaries

it's almost impossible to understand what I'm talking about. The assumptions that underpinned my life belong to another world. To my sons there is the acknowledgement that they might one day have wives who will want to compete for the right to be dedicated to their work. To my mother it's distressing. But for me, and for many of my generation, it's a tectonic shift.

Going to Antarctica is a long, arduous, incredibly rewarding journey. It takes effort, and organisation, and strength, and some courage. I've been lucky. I've been given the chance to live in and learn about this extraordinary ice-age continent.

But I've also grown, in myself. I'm pretty sure I'm too passive, too accepting, too much of my generation ever to have experienced the shift without the massive physical journey.

But thinking and writing about the change has unpacked a bit. I do believe that it is possible, at this age, even in the midst of accepted and familiar obligations, to give yourself the right to your own space once again. To reacquaint yourself with your original self – possibly adventurous, possibly independent, possibly creative. It's reasonable to adjust the balance.

And it can be done without having to live in a forty-bunk Antarctic scientific research station with slices of massive ice cliff collapsing and roaring into the sea outside your bedroom window.

PATRICIA MOBERLY

From the desk of the chairman

Some relax when they reach their sixties,
but that wasn't Patricia Moberly's way. She describes
what she did instead.

I said to Richard, my husband, the other morning that this is the first time in my life that I have ever felt happy about going to work in the morning and not particularly wanting to go on holiday – whereas while I was teaching, in my previous career, I would be counting the days.

I am chairman of the Guy's and St Thomas's National Health Service Trust, appointed after fifteen months as a member of the board. I retired in 1998 from my long-term full-time job as head of sixth form at a big London comprehensive school and had been looking around for job opportunities elsewhere in the public sector, so the opportunity to serve the combined trust was a god-send. I was on Westminster Bridge yesterday and I thought, 'I am just so lucky to work in such a wonderful place.' It is a wonderful job. It is so worthwhile. Every day is different.

There are two well-known hospitals now merged into a single organisation with 6500 staff. I work three and a half days a week. One day I may be chairing an appointment panel for a consultant post; another showing visitors around; another may be full of meetings concerned with various aspects of administration. I am determined that we concentrate first and foremost on the needs of patients, which is the reason for our existence, and that everyone, from chief executive to cleaner, feels a valued member of a team. There is much more variety than there was in teaching. I also spend a great deal of time out in the local community represent-ing the hospital trust and trying to interpret its policies and problems to others. The fascination of the job, for me, lies partly in the novelty of it after thirty-five years of teaching, but mostly in the wonderful people that I work with and try to lead.

That is what I enjoy most. The combination of academic skills, thinking and enquiring minds plus a genuine motivation to help, makes people much more interesting than if they just want to make money. Then there is the public-service ethos that welds the hospital community together. I was born at a time when it was difficult for a woman to go into politics, but in this job I can also use what skills I have to improve the lot of some people.

It was Africa that first got me interested in politics, when we went to live in Zambia a few years after we married. If you live in a community where half lives on one side of the street and the rest on the other, you can't be semi-detached. I joined the United National Independence Party – the UNIP. The society there was very unfair. I felt very uncomfortable. We lived a fairly normal life at home but at school the children picked up the attitudes of the other white children. My eldest daughter was aged six when I told her to pick up her things off the floor; she said, 'That is a black person's job.' I said, 'That's it. We are going back to England.' We

could not protect them from it because that was the kind of school they went to. We were there three and a half years. I was twenty-three when we went with three children under four and came back with four under six.

But I had already glimpsed the inequalities of life back in England. I was a student in Liverpool and it was the first time I saw children without any shoes. I was very surprised. It was an unusually interesting place to be, particularly given my father's views. My father was quite active in the Tory party. He was the agent in the village. There was always a lot of the *Daily Telegraph* at home! It's sad that I was never able to communicate with my father and persuade him that maybe some things in the Labour party were worthwhile.

I did not actually do anything political while I was in Africa other than join the party. But I did when I came back. I was very active with the anti-apartheid movement, serving on its National Executive Committee. I was sort of in the front line. Campaigning for racial justice has been, and still is, the most important cause of my adult life. I believe that the history of the twentieth century was shaped profoundly by racial hatred, intolerance and prejudice, and that each of us needs to aim for greater justice in the twenty-first century and to try by example to pass this message on to our children.

I had gone to university for no particular reason. Towards the end of my course I went to the careers office and said, 'I will do anything but be a teacher,' but they said, 'That is all you can be.' When we went to Zambia, I was a bit bored so I taught in an African school, which was set up by the mining community for future black management.

I continued my teaching career when I got home from Africa. It was something that I could fit into my calendar. At first I taught part-time when the children were small. We needed the money. Richard was a priest. I didn't want to persuade him to do anything else because that was what he wanted to do. We could have lived without me working but with extreme difficulty. We have never wanted holidays but we did want children and cats and a car, and it is very difficult to manage without a second income. I know very few clergy who have no second income. Then, when they retire, the money is quite dreadful.

I loved the school in Africa but less so in England. I just did not like going into the building. Perhaps it was because I was very unhappy myself at school. But on the whole schools are not particularly enjoyable institutions. I tried to make school interesting and tolerable for the children. I don't think that children together are very nice to each other. I can't bear to see distressed kids. But I must not denigrate teaching. In thirty-five years I taught some brilliant kids and I have learned a lot myself. I 'did' a lot of books. When I left teaching I was just beginning to understand *Paradise Lost*. Just beginning to.

Today I am much happier, oh, far happier. I am still a magistrate. I love my job at the hospital. I have made people aware of choices. I have helped people to think around issues of fairness, like how to behave to black staff. I have brought a new experience to my job and they respect the fact I have been a teacher all these years.

There is one other good thing about being sixty with no more teaching: I now have a lot more time for friends and for myself. I have had various car accidents and a lot of illness, but it is of little consequence. The one thing you do not want to do is to clobber everyone else with it and talk about it. I keep my ailments to myself and get on with the work I love.

PAULINE BEWICK

In full bloom

For many, the sixties are a time, not for change, but for a full flowering of one's early talents. Pauline Bewick, a hugely successful Irish artist, looks back on how she came to be where and what she is today.

A rose in full bloom conjures up, for me, a picture of petals falling off one by one, leaving the centre petals attached for longer. The analogy being that the core of one's personality shows up more strongly when one is in full bloom than at any other time of life. If the rose were aware, it would be conscious of letting go. One petal might, a little sadly, represent smooth skin, shiny hair, feeling sexy, being attractive. Other petals I willingly let go: self-consciousness, for instance, and insecurity. However, once the petals have fallen off, the very core of the person is left and that becomes very sharp indeed. I know this from my paintings. I have developed a free feeling allowing me to express things in a very clear manner.

I'm painting larger, with more excitement, and time has brought a wide audience to appreciate my work, but age liberates me from trying to please anybody but myself. As a young person, if given a commission it was difficult to get into the mind of the person who made the request. Now I translate the request into my own way of thinking. The commission then becomes far stronger than my younger approach.

I used to think that sixty was incredibly old. But now, in my mid-sixties, I don't feel incredibly old – just occasionally. In fact, when rested I feel incredibly young.

Looking back, I suspect that my early life was hugely important in shaping my art and personality. My mother, Alice May Graham, was born the youngest of a middle-class family in New-castle-upon-Tyne. She became a tearaway. Her free spirit rubbed off on me. She didn't believe in education and would say things like 'What do you want to know all that stuff for, filling up your head?' and 'That's all past and done with', if I should ask a question about my father. I was two and a half when my father died. We were living on the farm that we were given in return for fostering two children whose parents had died of TB. We stayed happily on that farm for eight years or so. My sister went to the convent in Kenmare, along with Lucy and Michael, and I attended the small two-roomed country school called Dauros where my teacher Miss Murphy said things like 'I know you can't spell, Pauline, but you're very good at drawing. Will you draw a bird for us on the blackboard?' She and my mother were my confidence builders. They made me feel extremely proud of this one gift.

The things that followed were harder to tackle but didn't damage me. For instance, my mother's admiration for A. S. Neill prompted her to bring me back to England and enrol me in two different progressive schools. The teachers were eccentric, we called them by their first names; the pupils often emotionally disturbed, from difficult backgrounds. That's not to say that the teachers weren't good, my favourite being Dorothy Higgins, the art teacher. We were allowed to choose our classes; I always chose art with Dorothy. She loved trees and would rave on about the knots and nobbles and branches. We would go out together daily, drawing and painting.

When I was a young teenager, the family returned to Ireland to live in a boat, a workman's hut, a hotel gate lodge and finally in a caravan parked on black cinders behind an advertisement board in Kilmainham, Dublin. I would open the door of the advertisement board, step out of the tin of beans and go to the art school. These years were magic. Bare feet and sackcloth skirts, flirting, dancing, a job in a nightclub singing, happy swapping talk while sitting on the hot pipes of the art school. In the art school I would stick to the classes drawing David's nose or the Venus de Milo but one day I sneaked into the life classes and made myself invisible, staying there for the rest of my term. When I got home in the evenings I still painted but in my own style with poster paints and inks.

My mother encouraged me more than any woman could, single-mindedly saying, 'Don't wash up, you paint' and things like 'That is marvellous, you are a genius'. Until I was about thirty-five and she said something that shocked me, 'I won't go to your Exhibition, I'm through with art, its like fiddling while Rome burns.' 'You should be out there doing something for the world.' 'Why don't you read Krishnamurti?' I took till now to get over her turnabout. She died in 1979.

In actual fact, my mother not only kept the drawings I had done from the age of two and a half in Kenmare, drawings like the first wedding I ever saw, paintings of a cattle fair in Kenmare and also the pupils and teachers of the progressive schools, but she also held on to my teenage works. Consequently I too kept a collection until I was fifty. Then I had a retrospective exhibition in the Guinness Hop Store in Dublin, and in Irish museums, of works from the age of two and a half to fifty comprising 1500 individual pieces.

With all the freedom my mother gave me, I felt instinctively that it would be harmful to be too free with my crushes. I fell in love about four times. Each differed but none had the intelligence, wit, love of nature and security that my now husband has for me. Throughout our life together, Pat has had an amazing calming effect on me, soothing my work and my obsessional nature and pointing out that 'the brent geese have arrived' or suggesting 'let's go to the Beckett play' or taking me, when we were very young, to the Continent. The other affairs were with wild men, totally unreliable but exciting at the time, making my life rounder and answering many questions for me and my friends.

It was Pat who persuaded me to have children. The world seemed such an awful place to bring fresh life into. I felt I would love them too much to see them witness suffering, wars and turmoil. I also worried that I might stop creating pictures once I started to create babies. Pat made me realise that I must be selfish to be happy and boy, did it work. Our first child, Poppy, was born when I was thirty-one. I adored her and found the whole experience awful and yet wonderful. My pictures throughout illustrated these two emotions, pictures like a woman with her head in the sand with her children, the title being *I May Get My Bum Blown Off But I Bury My Head in the Sand*. I was then persuaded by Pat that it wasn't fair to have just one so we had our darling Holly four years later. Both are now successful artists. Having children cocooned me against the rest of the world. I became totally engrossed in the business of loving and bringing them up. Now that they are both adults and have children of their own, the outside world has become more in focus for me.

As for my grandchildren, talk about a rose in full bloom! It's a bonus that I had never thought about. I feel as if I've lived over a hundred years. It's so amazing to witness these new lives developing in front of my eyes and the joy of not having to change nappies or be with them non-stop is huge. The wisdom that emanates from their young minds is thrilling to witness.

I think that I have acquired an intelligent wisdom through no effort of my own, something that gets me through my whole life with no regrets. If I have changed over the years I can only think, apart from the physical part, that it is for the better. I am calmer and grateful that I've got this far. Spirituality is a question that doesn't fill me with angst. I am quite relaxed and may discover there is a God, or that Darwin was right, or that it is to dust we return.

I can say now, in my sixties, that I feel totally fulfilled.

PENELOPE LYNDON-STANFORD

My gap year

It can be devastating when your mother dies and your children have all left home. Penelope Lyndon-Stanford decided it was a good time to take her gap year and travel round the world.

I am sixty-two and have just come back from travelling round the world by myself for nine months, with only a backpack for luggage. I went first to India and then Thailand, Burma now Myanmar, Hong Kong, China, Bali, Australia, New Zealand and North America. I was going to go on to South America, but I was in the United States on 11 September. I was sitting in a bar in New Mexico that day with other people, all strangers, glued to the television, watching as they showed the twin towers coming down, over and over again. Suddenly it did not seem right any more that I should be travelling and enjoying myself. All I wanted at that moment was to be at home with my family.

My mother had died just before Christmas the year before. I was devastated. She had been my friend and confidante for most of my grown-up life. After her death I felt that there was nothing left for me to do. It was the end of an era. I was now the older generation and had, I thought, fulfilled all my uses in this world. I had brought up four children, and waited until my mother died; it was now time for me to die. I began to think that in the old days, when you had done all this, you probably did die.

It is difficult to put into words how I felt. Part of me was now free – with all my children grown up and with children of their own. I could do what I wanted. But I had spent most of my life looking after people, with never enough time for myself, not that I felt I needed it. I now felt useless. I had to find out who I was. Whatever I did it had to be frightening, to stop me thinking. I suppose in a way I almost wanted to change myself, or at least not to feel or think any more. All the young seemed to have had 'Gap Years'; why shouldn't I go away and see what would happen? I felt it had to be some sort of challenge so that I could start living again. I could not just give up. Nowadays we all live so much longer. There is a life after children now, a space where we can have some time to ourselves to find out what and who we are.

I was born in India at the beginning of the Second World War, and spent the first eighteen months there. In 1940 my mother and I came back to England on a ship. When the war broke out my mother was asked if she would like to stay on in India where at that time they thought we would all be safer. She said she wanted to go home, however bad it was in England. My father, who was in the army, was by this time in England waiting for us. She told me later how every night she packed a little survival bag in case we got torpedoed. Apparently we were meant to be travelling on the boat that left before the one that we were on. The first boat was torpedoed, but my father in England kept saying, 'No, I know that they won't be on that boat.' He adored my mother. I

found myself thinking about what my mother had said when 11 September happened in the USA. I was on my way to New York and all I felt was that I did not want to get trapped anywhere away from home if there was going to be a war.

I spent my early life following my parents around the world like so many of my generation. Eventually I went to a convent school, then on to do a secretarial training, and for a short time became a secretary, which I hated. I had one boss who used to say to me, 'Lift your skirt a bit higher, Miss Brown.' He always made me feel so bad.

I married and had four beautiful children, three girls and a boy. My husband then went to work in Italy and I joined a friend who had just started a catering business. We worked together for about four years. Then we divided the business and both went our separate ways. Some time after this my husband, the father of my children, and I also went our separate ways when we got divorced. Of course, at the time both these events were not as simple or as pain-free as they now seem. Thank goodness our memory for unhappiness is not as good as it is for the happy times.

I carried on with my catering business until about 1995, when it started to run down. The television company with whom I had my biggest contract was taken over, so I knew my days were numbered. I had to think of something else to do. I started a small Bed and Breakfast business, after some good advice from a close friend of mine who said that one should always begin a new venture before the last one has completely run down. But I still do some catering, which I have always found very exciting.

I now have four grandchildren and another on the way, as well as my four children. Sometimes I feel that all these people I love will overwhelm me and I will never be myself. That is why I found travelling alone so fantastic. I met new and wonderful people. There was the single American man in China who was seventy-five and had just had a triple heart bypass operation. He was hugely enthusiastic and lively, walking up the Great Wall of China and trekking down the Yellow Mountains in Yangshu. Or the woman who travelled round China with a colostomy bag. Anyone who has travelled in China knows that this is not an easy feat. I shared a room with her for a month. She never complained.

Then there was the Moslem taxi driver in Bhopal whom I had hired for the day to take me to see the caves with old Indian carvings in them. He brought his thirteen-year-old daughter with him. I had not realised at the time how far away from anywhere it was. Right up in the mountains and very lonely, I only saw one other man there with his dog. I would have been very frightened had it not been for the young girl who spoke good English and stayed very close to me while her father walked some way back from us. I was impressed by his thoughtfulness. Or the seventy-two-year-old Canadian woman who travelled by herself around India every year for three months. I asked her if she would like to come to Burma with me and immediately she replied, 'Why not?' These individuals, and many more like them, have made me realise that people can surprise you, once you get to know them. I realised that my life until then had been quite sheltered in many ways.

I did frighten myself at times, but not as much as I thought I would. It was probably more frightening thinking about it before I went, which is what I believe got me through the first year after my mother died. Those nine months travelling by myself have made me feel more confident in myself and widened my horizons. I now realise that life can continue to be fun, even as an older woman.

When I got back home from my nine months away, I found that I had got back to the usual horrors that seem to happen to all women. We had rats in the cellar, the roof was leaking, and my son's girlfriend had crashed the front and back of my car. The battery was flat and I had to keep getting jump-starts. My plan is to write, something I have always wanted to do but never seemed to have the time for. I just hope that I can manage to start before I get bogged down again in domesticity.

What I have discovered is that you don't have to do anything very amazing to reactivate your life. Just try. You will change, inspire and help yourself and other people, while having a fantastic time. In particular I can recommend anyone to go round the world, whatever their age, and preferably by themselves, to realise how lovely and interesting most people are.

Perpetual motion!

Would you decide to run a stall in the local markets as the mainstay of your sixties? Pippa Weir and her husband did just that but, as she explains, life, for her, is a never-ending adventure – which doesn't stop just because you turn sixty.

In my sixtieth year my husband and I took on one more challenge. This time it was selling cheese at local markets. It was our biggest challenge so far, but very rewarding. It's amazing how quickly you can learn a fair amount about a subject that you knew only a little about before starting. The business became a great success but, at sixty-two, getting up at 4 a.m. in the cold and dark did not seem so appealing. If only we had started it ten years earlier. We sold it and moved on.

Looking back, the cheese business was just the last in what had been a long succession of wildly different enterprises. In my sixties, my guess is that it will be the same, only slower – and less early in the mornings! Life has been a continuous adventure thus

far and I see no reason for it to stop just because I turned sixty. This is only possible, of course, if you have your health. Sadly, so many of my friends have not survived their sixties. My husband and I feel that we have the chance for more changes and challenges, to do much that we could not do if we were tied to a job or were ill.

It was 8.30 a.m. on 4 September 1939 when I came into the world – the seventh war baby in Cambridge. My mother had spent 3 September in the nursing home on Midsummer Common, listening to the news that we had declared war on Germany. Inevitably, she wondered what sort of world she had brought me into. I was christened Philippa (lover of horses) but always called Pippa. It was not an easy time for my mother. My father was in West Africa where he was a civil engineer building roads and bridges. He did not see me until I was two and a half. My mother ran a photo printing office, which she had started about six years before I was born, as a temporary occupation while my father was away. She was still running this into her early eighties – longevity and busyness must be in my genes!

My teens were occupied with horses until, at seventeen and still at school, I met my first husband, who was in his first year at King's College. We were married three years later and moved straight to Maisons Laffitte – a racehorse town just outside Paris. Daunting for a twenty-year-old who only had bad O-level French. During this time I continued riding by exercising racehorses. We were there for three years before returning to England, where I had two sons. Sadly, after seventeen years, this marriage ended. I think we just grew apart. Twenty is certainly too young to get married but, in the 1960s, you had little choice if you wanted to live together.

Three years later I got married again to someone seven years younger. He had also married too young. Our big common interest was sailing. Every weekend was spent racing. For the first seven years, Peter continued as before – running his family shoe business while I went on with my secretarial work. But by now we were both feeling the need for a more exciting challenge. Both my sons had finished school, Nick was in the band of the Life Guards and Anthony was at university. We sold the house in Sussex and bought a very small cottage in Suffolk – somewhere to put our furniture and to come back to during the winters. We were free, free to indulge ourselves with new challenges and enterprises. We decided to spend two years running flotillas in Yugoslavia. This was followed by three years running our own charter yacht in Turkey. All this was fun but I'm not sure which was the harder – trying to direct people from a ship's radio when they were lost and could only see 'a rock' or to keep smiling at difficult guests on board.

But by now I am heading towards fifty – another turning point. The boat was sold and replaced by a magnificent chateau in

France, which we planned to run as chambres d'hôtes. We enjoyed renovating the chateau, even when the local mayor told us a previous owner had committed suicide there – and we did find human bones in the attic!

Somehow France did not fulfil our dreams, although we did live in a beautiful house. As one of my friends said, 'This must be it. Where do you go from here?' It was, however, in the wrong part of the country. Too quiet in the winter and too busy with guests in the summer. But we do go back occasionally and peer over the wall! We returned to England after three years, to Orford in Suffolk and an enormous 1930s house with wonderful views, but in need of a lot of renovation. But we needed to work.

Our next venture was a small yacht chandlery and a boat running river trips. The trips were fun for a couple of years but did become repetitive. So we sold that business and concentrated on the two local ferry services we had started. Working together went well, we found, as long as we each had our specific roles. The only downside is that there is not a great deal new to discuss in the evenings. Perhaps that is why we are always planning something new.

Eight years later, at the age of fifty-nine, we took on the next and latest challenge – selling cheese at local markets. This became a great success – if only we had started it ten years earlier! Just before we embarked on this venture we had taken part in a rally from London to Cape Town, driving through twenty-four countries in a Landrover. Africa is a continent with so many different faces. That trip gave us the feeling that we will always want to see changes in our life. Travelling gives you a great taste of freedom and the realisation that, to be interesting, life must always present a challenge.

And so we decided to sell up once again – business and house have now both gone and our next adventure is about to begin. What next, we ask? Will it be Africa – a place we love so much – or

France, or a combination of both? We still have two of the five dogs we once owned and so they do have a say in the decisions. For the moment we have decided to buy a house in France. Not a chateau, this time, but a barn in need of renovation. This will take a few years to do. Maybe we will then buy another one and do the same thing. We will still be free to take off with the dogs and camp again – something else we have gone back to after many years. Life never stands still, even in one's sixties.

I am not ready to 'retire'. I still feel that we will, one day, go to Africa. It is a continent so full of possibilities – I could become young again there. We can never know how much more life we may have but at least we now have the time to do all the little things that we could never do before. I did think, once, that my tombstone would have engraved on it 'there is never time' but now there will be and we are going to enjoy it to the full.

A time for pruning

Would you accept a friend's offer of life counselling? Prue Leith did so reluctantly but describes what then happened.

I started in the food business as a raw South African with no money. I used to make pâté in my bedsitter for pubs and cook lunches three days a week for a firm of solicitors. Thirty years later it had grown to an annual turnover of £14 million and a staff of 350.

I sold the business when I was 55 for the usual reasons: it was doing well and I wanted more time for other things. But I was also conscious that cautious old age might be setting in. I felt I was beginning to hold the business back. Managers would come to me and say, 'I've had this great idea . . .' and I'd start worrying that it would take too much capital, endanger my pension and the children's inheritance etc. The restaurant and catering world is for entrepreneurs and adventurers, and maybe I was losing it?

I sold the contract catering company, the party catering business and Leith's School of Food and Wine, but hung on to Leith's Restaurant. I had the idea that I might have withdrawal symptoms with no business at all to run. But within months I was having such a good time doing all sorts of other things that I sold the restaurant too – to Caroline Waldegrave who had been the principal of the school for twenty years and was now its owner. It pleased me that the staff would all stay. And my husband (my chairman and finance director) had negotiated 'dining rights', so I could still eat wonderful Leith's food for free without a badly ironed napkin or over-salty sauce being my problem. Bliss!

About this time I had a call from a woman friend, Peta, who had recently started a business advising senior executives faced with early retirement or redundancy on how to manage their lives. As a management consultant working in outplacement, she'd noticed that top business people were terrific at company strategy, succession planning, long-term plans, risk assessment etc., but did none of these things in their own lives and were unable to cope when disaster struck. She said she wanted to help me make sense of the rest of my life. I was outraged.

'I'm fine,' I said. 'I'm chairing the RSA, I've got a good portfolio of non-exec and not-for-profit jobs, I'm playing a lot of tennis, I'm happily married. I don't need counselling for God's sake.' The very word counselling makes me uneasy, with overtones of woolly dependency and touchy feely self-indulgence. Peta pleaded and argued, and eventually won by saying, 'Look, you're my mate. I need a high-profile female for my brochure.' I agreed to six hour-long sessions.

For the first two, Peta said I sat with my arms folded, looking hostile. But by session three I was hooked. Talking about yourself for an hour is quite an ego trip and I found myself telling her things I'd never told anyone, like that I'd always wanted to write a novel, but thought I lacked the talent.

'What would you say if someone said to you they'd always wanted to be a cook, but lacked the talent?' she asked.

'I'd tell them to go on a course and find out,' I replied.

'Exactly,' she said. 'So why not do a novel-writing course?'

I told her I'd had to turn down an offer from a South African consortium of restaurant and lodge keepers to open a Prue Leith College in South Africa, training young people for the restaurant industry. I longed to do it, but would need at least two weeks a year to go there and I just didn't have time. I told her I wanted to go on holiday with my son and my daughter, but one at a time, just the two of us. Family hols are great, but my children were now in their early twenties and I felt I was losing touch with them.

I told her that I wanted to revive some friendships with women all these years of work and children had made me neglect. I wanted to go walking. I wanted to take tennis lessons. I wanted to sing in tune . . . dreams and desires came tumbling out. Peta made me look down my list of appointments, jobs, consultancies, quangos. She made me put a line through all the ones I thought of with a groan: meetings I did not enjoy, organisations I'd agreed to help out of duty or because some friend had leant on me, committees that were talking shops. She was ruthless. I dumped a lot of stuff.Next she suggested I just put a line through a week in my diary every two or three months. Then I could use that space for all the things I wanted to do. And so on.

I have now walked in South Africa, Spain, New England, Italy and Morocco, usually with one or other of those women friends. I have been to Hong Kong and China with my son. I'm going to Argentina with my daughter. I've joined a tennis club. I'm learning to sing. I've been on a novel-writing course and a script-writing one. I've got a TV script in development and two novels published, with another one to come. The Prue Leith College in South Africa is thriving, with ninety students enrolled, many of them from poor black backgrounds.

I've accepted some fascinating jobs – I chair the first private company to manage failing state schools under contract: King's College for Technology and the Arts in Guildford. We have three schools so far, all now doing very well. I also chair the British Food Trust and I'm deeply involved with Training for Life, a charity trying to help young people with huge problems: of homelessness, drugs, lack of education etc. We hope to build a training restaurant in Soho where they can be given a job and help at the same time. If it's fashionable and fun, we reckon it will both help the young people and make some money for the charity.

But I suppose my greatest pleasure has been my involvement with the RSA. Its full title is the Royal Society for the Encouragement of Arts, Manufactures and Commerce, with a mission 'to embolden enterprise, to enlarge science, to refine art, to improve our manufactures and to extend our commerce'. In short, to fix society!

But to go back a bit: I had for many years been interested in education. I had seen so many young people, written off by their teachers and maybe even their parents, arrive in our kitchens with no ambition other than to earn a wage; sent there by the job centre with the tacit message that they were only good for washing-up. Given a disciplined environment, a good head chef who expected them to succeed and who encouraged them to learn, miracles would happen. Young men who had been hopeless at school would find they could add up, could work in a team, could make beautiful food, could meet a deadline.

In time I became the chairman of the RSA and led the programme Focus on Food, a five-year campaign (hugely supported by Waitrose) to get food education taken seriously in schools. Working in 2000 schools, we support teachers with materials and a progamme to ensure hands-on practical cooking. There's also an RSA fellowship studying the social benefits of good food education and a massive 'Cooking Bus' that tours the country teaching children *and* teachers.

The RSA also gave me the chance to lead the initiative to get the plinth in Trafalgar Square, empty for 150 years, used to display contemporary British Art. It took five years of lobbying, form-filling, fund-raising and negotiation, but we did it! My problem is that I am genuinely interested in almost everything. So the RSA, with its wide brief, suits me down to the ground.

All this makes me sound dreadfully solemn and virtuous. The truth is that I have breakfast in bed every weekend, lovingly brought by my husband, I spend most weekends gardening, cooking and eating. I guess my secret, if it is a secret, is energy. I do have a lot of that. And I only do things that really interest me. Every now and again I resign from things I no longer enjoy, and thank my stars that, at sixty-two, I still get offered wonderful things to do. I'm definitely falling off the business perch a bit. But working for charities is just as interesting as commercial business. Often you are doing exactly the same thing: in effect running a business, but with more interesting problems, like having no money at all. That beats worrying all the time about your shareholders or the City analysts.

Learning by living

Sometimes the whole of life can seem to be a preparation for one's sixties. Dame Rennie Fritchie describes how she came to be where she is today, with more to come.

A t the time of writing, I am Commissioner for England, Scotland, Wales and by separate order in council for Northern Ireland. I am appointed by the Queen and Privy Council to hold government departments and ministers to account on behalf of the public for some 12,500 public appointments and to encourage diversity and transparency. My first office was based in Whitehall in the Treasury building. I stood in the corridor outside the heavy oak door with my name on it looking down the corridor to the office of the Chancellor of the Exchequer and I thought 'These *are* the corridors of power. These are the very corridors and here I am. Who would have thought it?'

There was little in my childhood to suggest that I would end up here. I was born in a small town on the east coast of Scotland in

1942 right in the middle of a war. My mother, my sister and I lived with my grandparents until well after my father had returned from the war and we reached the top of the list for a council house of our own. Soon afterwards it was Southern Rhodesia for three years, back to Scotland and then to Gloucestershire, where my father retired from the RAF and bought the tenancy of the Royal George, a country hotel.

The hotel was the reason that I left school before my sixteenth birthday. It seemed much more exciting to work there than continue to study. In those days higher education was not something thought of as desirable for girls in our family. The Royal George was also the village pub so we were at the heart of village life right away. Here we had many adventures and a lot of hard work and, if we didn't travel, life came to us.

It was here that I met my husband Don, an American Chief Petty Officer based at GCHQ in Cheltenham. He was a quiet American, a good bit older than I was and I fell for him. My parents didn't approve but stubbornly I married him anyway. After some time he was posted to Turkey. At nineteen and a half, after six months apart, I flew to join him. I was eight months pregnant and had never flown before. When I arrived he was away on business. A week after he got back, I was sent several hundred miles to Ankara for the birth of our son Charles Eric. I had to learn about being a mother very fast. We lived in a Turkish village about an hour and a half from the base where Don worked. Conditions were very primitive. We had no newspapers, television, radio or many general amenities. I often think of this episode in my life as the time when I learned to think, how to figure things out and understand them and how to change my own attitude to make the most of things, to think positively. I learned to be resourceful. I liked Turkey and the Turkish people. I had become used to the pace of life, so was not really prepared for the USA – our next posting.

During my seven years in the States I experienced the Washington riots, the murders of Martin Luther King and Robert Kennedy, and the Vietnam War. I had four more babies, lost three and gave healthy birth to my second son, Andrew.

Our next posting to England came at a very welcome time. I was ready to come home and see my wider family again. My marriage had not been a happy one and after eighteen months back in England I came to realise that this was the best it was going to be and it wasn't good enough for any of us. I left home with two children aged eight and six, plus the dog (then in heat), with only £30, no other income, no place to live, no career to go back to and no qualifications. It was probably the riskiest thing I have ever done. But we survived. And I learned a huge lesson about fear and taking risks. This was the toughest jump of our lives with absolutely no guarantee of success, and yet it was the right thing to do. I learned that you could begin again and knit  together a new life with very little in the way of resources, so long as you have personal values, inner strength and the willingness and ability to create options and try them.

Finding a place to live and a job, any job, was my first task. Building a new life in Gloucestershire was next. I worked full time in administrative roles. Not having the technical skills to be a secretary meant that I could fit more easily into a range of different jobs. I kept volunteering, expanding my role and learning new skills. I challenged the systems. After all, I had a family to feed so the luxury of a dented ego and giving up after a failure was not available to me. Moving into a training role seemed a natural step.

I had loved learning on training courses and I was therefore enthusiastic about encouraging others to learn too. It also seemed natural to focus on women's development. I began to write articles, co-wrote books and was awarded a German Marshall Fellowship to compare and contrast equal opportunities programmes in the US and UK. I felt there was nothing that was impossible to tackle. If there is a sadness from this time it's that it wasn't possible to develop and sustain a long-term relationship. I even wrote a verse about it.

Some day my prince will come they said when I was small.
Brave and true, kind and strong, handsome dark and tall.
I'm only a woman doing my best, waiting for my turn.
Supporting, listening, smiling, nodding, knowing I have much to learn.
Only men could do the tough stuff, telling others what to do.
I just ran the home, the kids, my job, filled the larder, cleaned the loo.
Along the way I met some stars, pretenders who didn't tarry.
And then one day I realised I'd become the man I wanted to marry!

After working as a trainer for some years I began a new chapter as a consultant, first in an international consultancy and then starting up my own company. It was around this time that the 300 Group began campaigning for more women to be selected for public appointments and to expand what was then known as the list of the 'great and the good'. Through their work my name was one of many that went forward for consideration. After a six-month wait I was appointed as the part-time chair of Gloucester Health Authority, still continuing with my consultancy work.

And so began a new and exciting decade of portfolio working. I learned that to be of service is a real privilege and that work can be challenging, worthwhile and enjoyable. I learned that I was good at strategy, at seeing the big picture and at sustaining a productive and supportive culture. I moved several times in the NHS during that decade taking on bigger jobs and playing small national roles. Ultimately I chaired one of eight NHS Regions, the South and West. I also continued doing my consultancy, charity work and writing books.

A personal tragedy struck me and my family in 1991 when my son Eric, then twenty-nine, was knocked down by a hit-and-run driver and left for five hours to die in a ditch. Nothing can be worse than this, nothing. The world is never the same again. Eric left behind a wife and daughter, Laura, then just eighteen months old. Taking time out to grieve, then continuing on, seemed the best way forward. However, in 1995 I decided I wanted more time with my mother who was growing older and to see more of my granddaughter, so I resigned from the NHS in March 1996.

I was made a Dame Commander in January 1996, which was an enormous surprise and a great honour. In my family the only dames we knew of were pantomime dames in funny clothes, so in keeping with that tradition my son Andrew bought me a diamanté tiara and a Harley Davidson leather waistcoat with THE DAME in metal studs on the back! To his disappointment I didn't wear it to the Palace!

After three years of focusing mainly on consultancy work I saw an advertisement for the role of Commissioner for Public Appointments. It was a part-time role regulating the process of making public appointments like the one I had held in the NHS. I applied and, to my surprise and delight, was appointed in 1999.

Looking back, it seems to me that my life has always been a series of episodes with a range of choices and changes. As one phase drew to a close another started. Within these episodes there have been redefining moments when everyday certainty disappeared and it became necessary to re-imagine myself and my future. I have and am having a good life, one that I never expected, and yet every now and then I wonder just what my next big adventure will be. At sixty I am now ready for anything the world can throw at me.

ROSEMARY HAMILTON

Happy singleton

What is it like to be sixty and single?
Rosemary Hamilton has never married – from choice.
Now that she is sixty should she feel sorry for herself?
Not at all, she says. Life is full, with more to come.

'**W**ho waits upon the when and how / Remains forever in the rear.' These words by the poet Wilbur Dick Nesbit sum up my approach to life. I have always tried to live up to them.

At boarding school I was voted 'the girl most likely to get married first'. Here I am, some forty-five years further down the line, indubitably single, evidently content, a successful decorator and designer, and still with several goals in my sights.

I had no inkling, then, that I would one day run my own interior design business for thirty years. I had always wanted to be an architect, but when I left school in the mid-Fifties, the idea of doing a seven-year training was not even considered. It was hard to know what one might be doing in seven months' time, let alone seven years. Unusually for those days, my mother had read English at Oxford in the 1920s. In my day only 'blue stockings' went to university and, after the ubiquitous secretarial course, we were all expected to get jobs and flats in London.

I am one of the last daughters of the Raj. My grandfather was in the Indian Army and in 1928 my father, fed up with life in a bank in the City, boarded a boat bound for Calicut in India to work for one of the trading firms in the East. He moved on to Malaya (as it then was) and, while on holiday in Singapore, drove up to Flagstaff House to leave a courtesy visiting card. His first sight of my mother was of a girl sitting on the veranda with each elbow in half a grapefruit, whitening her skin. They duly married and set up home in Penang where I was born and brought up.

Like all European children, my brother, sister and I came back to England in due course to be educated. I felt rather sorry for my school friends who did not know the lure of the East, had not seen dawn shimmer on a tropical island or tasted a fresh coconut. After school, I worked in London and also travelled the world with a girlfriend, working in the States to earn enough money to go on to the next stage. Thankfully, in the 1960s an English accent was highly valued and at one time I was selling English hand-made leather golf gloves to the Americans.

In 1970 I took the decision to enter the decorating world. My first client was my then boyfriend who, in lieu of payment, gave me a Kenwood mixer – I still have the mixer but not the man. Besides being a decorator, I play the part of mediator, psychiatrist, hand-holder and decision-maker on behalf of my clients. I have often been driven crazy by them, but it is never a dull life. I have met fascinating people I would never have encountered and travelled all over the world, decorating and designing houses and offices.

At the same time I was able to take advantage of my single status to get a mortgage and to invest in a property market where

you could double your money by buying a wreck, doing it up and selling it, ready for the next venture. I'll never forget the look on the face of my rather avuncular bank manager in those days when I asked him about getting a mortgage. 'But you will get married and have children,' he countered. 'So are you sure?'

I had never been more sure. I had always dreamt of living in Belgravia and I reached my dream flat in Eaton Place in four hops. I became heavily involved in the Interior Decorators and Designers Association, being on the Council for six years and then chairman for the regulatory two-year appointment. I was the first woman chairman ever. Again I had the opportunity of meeting new people and travelling to different countries.

About ten years ago I was called for Jury Service. Being a one-woman business, this was most disruptive and I dreaded the time I would have to consign to it. The cases were fairly minor, youths nicking radios, shoplifting, etc. I had never been inside a court before and was usually voted Leader of the Jury to announce the verdict. What I was totally unprepared for was the adverse attitude of the police. All they wanted was a conviction. The jurors felt that the police were often biased in their statements and, I regret to say, they sometimes appeared to be stretching the truth. The immediate response of the jurors was to give a 'Not Guilty' verdict despite privately thinking the opposite.

The stand of the police really vexed me and I decided to dig further. I started in a very small way by becoming chairman of our local Neighbourhood Watch. I also joined the local Working Sector Group and am now doing my two-year stint as chairman. This is the direct liaison group with the police and the public. I am also involved in the Police/Community Consultative Group that involved the local council.

Five years ago I joined a small group of local residents with the sole idea of raising money from the businesses and traders in the area to set up a CCTV project. Of course, there are many such schemes but ours is one of the very few in this country where the cameras are monitored in the police station by police officers, twenty-four hours a day. We raised nearly £500,000 and with this were able to buy enough cameras to cover two important areas of crime. We had some opposition from civil liberties groups, but mostly the cameras have been well received and have produced some encouraging results. While they will never replace the policeman on the beat, with the present low number of officers, they certainly provide some useful help.

So over the last few years I have met and got to know the police in a professional capacity and have joined them at social events, farewell parties and the like. I have seen them in a different light. They work under the most difficult circumstances, due to financial restrictions and lack of manpower. They attend the groups mentioned above in their free time. I continue to be amazed at what they are asked to put up with and I feel they need all the help and support the public can give them.

Having now passed sixty, how does one attain the measured balance of one's life? I am still working. I decided to cut down by only working for existing clients. My original clients are downsizing and their children are upgrading so, between them, I still seem to be kept fairly busy.

I am often asked how I feel about not getting married or having children. Many years ago I went to a Chinese fortune teller in Singapore who told me I was going to have eight children. Ridiculous, I thought. However, I do have five nephews and nieces and three godchildren. Both my brother and sister and their families lived abroad for many years and sent their children back to school in England, so I used to see a lot of them. I always thought it was the perfect arrangement – I would have them out from school when they were on their best behaviour and then send them back to their parents for the holidays. Spending time with them keeps me up to date with what's going on in their world.

My parents were disappointed I never married but I always maintained better never to have married than to be miserable. However, as I grow older I realise that the most important thing is, as the French say, 'to be happy in your skin'. No one wants to listen to a moaning Minnie all day. Always have something to look forward to – even if it is only the next police meeting! Never say never.

ROSEMARY HOPKINS

A reinvented life

What happens when a new man enters your life in your late fifties when you thought that life was already full and fulfilling? Rosemary Hopkins explains how it changed her view of her sixties.

Over the past sixty years I have done a lot of reinventing, of imagining myself to be different and at times creating that difference, mostly by adopting different roles. As a teenager and in my twenties my dream was to be like other people, especially physically. In my thirties I became a wife, mother and yoga teacher. However, by the time I reached forty I was beginning to find a new energy.

I was brought up with the maxims 'Children should be seen and not heard', and 'Just to please me'. Like my favourite children's book character, Leo the Late Bloomer, I needed time, time to discover my own voice, authority and creativity. In my sixth decade I bloomed! This meant leaving a marriage of eighteen

years, making a new home for my children, acknowledging my gifts and becoming self-sufficient. Fitting in or belonging didn't seem so important any more. Intellectually I was continuing to grow, studying two university courses. Emotionally I was discovering depths and understandings during my counselling diploma that I had only vaguely encountered before. Physically, I was fit and strong.

My spiritual journey was more complicated. After a wide exploration of Eastern religions, I returned to the safety and comfort of my childhood Anglican faith. But this was to last only until the next discovery. Now I was more ready to go with what fitted me than how I fitted in. When opportunities to grow both spiritually and emotionally through the Jungian archetypes and the ancient teachings of indigenous peoples presented themselves, I was ready to respond.

I had a full and fulfilled life. I felt a sufficiency, freedom and creative energy that were new to me. My story could have ended there, happy with myself, my grown-up children, and ageing dogs and cat.

But the story didn't end there. In my late fifties I met and corresponded with – hundreds of e-mails – a remarkable man, an American living in London. From my home on the edge of a tiny village in Scotland, culturally he was a world away. He worked internationally and home was where he recovered between trips and did the laundry. Could I fit in? Did I want to put myself through another upheaval emotionally and physically? Certainly I was rusty sexually! But with Walt in my life, I was filled with a vibrant energy which burst out of me in joy and delight.

I had committed myself to making a difference in the world. I was counselling people; I was co-ordinating Traidcraft locally, working to alleviate poverty in the underdeveloped world. Suddenly I was being offered a different path, a chance to love and be loved, to embrace a life of travel and opportunities for further discoveries, and to do all this with a man who shared so many of my passions – nature, the arts, travel, and exploring ways of living more fully and in a relationship.

That was the challenge for me – to live well in a relationship and to make a commitment to this process. At our wedding we had three candles of different shades on the altar. We each lit one of the smaller ones to honour and celebrate all the gifts we brought to our marriage, and together we lit the central candle to honour and celebrate our shared gifts and our different gifts. All three candles burned brightly as we sang our way out of the church!

Life has been wonderful but it has also been difficult. The shared gifts were joyful. The different gifts at times have been painful. There were parts of me that I was willing to let go, but I did not want to lose the freedom and energy that I had discovered before meeting Walt. Just once I've said to him, 'You're blowing out my candle,' referring to the metaphor and the ritual we had created at our marriage ceremony. I had also made a talking stick, a tool of the Native American teachings of the Ehama Institute in California. When I needed to speak my truth and be heard I would pick it up. This proved a respectful and beautiful way to do this, laying down the stick once I had spoken, and being willing to listen if Walt wished to pick it up and speak.

Walt moved into my house. Territory proved confusing. I was able to be generous and yet felt the pain of loss. I gave him my bedroom to use as his study. I still miss the sunrises and the full moonlight. I kept so much of the house that eventually we agreed to make the sitting room a place that was ours rather than mine.

We gave ourselves a weekend to empty the room. A log fire had been installed and the painter had completed his task. We started putting books on the shelves and suddenly my tears began to flow. I could feel myself disappearing as the room changed. How would people know who I was? How could I be me in a room shared with another person? Yet as I voiced my sadness and fear, I knew that I was more visible now than I had ever been. I could indeed share the space with another, especially one who valued me. We hung our pictures in mixed clusters, and lovingly placed our precious things. The room grew and mellowed over that weekend and several weeks later my daughter congratulated us on what we had achieved. She reassured me that I was very present, as was Walt.

I also reinvented my working life, focusing on unpaid work with adult survivors of sexual abuse and on the supervision of bereavement counsellors and helpline workers. I became aware of a definite shift in my values. It is not enough to accommodate each other, it is important to trust greatness of spirit and to expand. This expansion has meant a fresh look at what I thought was a holistic approach to my life and work, and to realise how easy it is to focus on the pain, shame, blame issues, and to overlook the beauty and gifts of the person with whom I am in relationship. Through my spiritual growth and discovery of a more appreciative view of the world and all its creatures, I am beginning to move into another phase of reinvention.

And so it was that on 11 September 2001 I was with the women of Arana, which is a five-year Leadership Collaborative that I have joined in the United States and due to fly home from New York that night. Our closing circle was interrupted with these words: 'Take a deep breath, this is going to be hard to hear – America is under attack.' I felt a primal terror in my separation from my loved ones. I felt so small; the Atlantic seemed so huge and unfriendly.

The months that followed were very difficult for me as I met parts of myself that I had not encountered before. I began to weave them into myself and my marriage with increasing awareness of their significance. I realised how important it is to be explicit about loving and being loved. Discovering and reinventing myself goes on, stimulated by my deepening values of freedom, justice, non-violence and love.

In my sixty-second year, I believe I can make a difference, as a woman, wife, mother and, now, as a grandmother. I never knew my grandmothers and my mother was a remote grandmother to my children. So I am inventing my grandmotherhood with delight. My mother is responsible for a lot of who I am despite living on another continent. Throughout her life my mother ate the same food, wore the same style of clothes and lived in a house that hardly changed in the fifty years she was married to my father. I envy her stability, but I am not her. I will continue to embrace new ideas and new experiences with energy and passion, and will celebrate the challenge of living in a loving relationship with Walt.

SHIRLEY DANIELS

Dreams come true at sixty-five

*When you resign on principle as head teacher
at age fifty-eight you don't expect life to offer you an
even better opportunity in your sixties. Shirley Daniels
describes how her dreams came true in an
unexpected way.*

I write this sitting in a spacious bungalow with a large garden filled with bougainvillaea, hibiscus and jasmine. I came to Ras Al Khaimah in the United Arab Emirates as deputy principal (head of secondary) of the international school at the invitation of the owner, HH Sheikh Saud, and the chair of governors. The invitation was a total surprise. I was out there on a holiday while Jacquie, my old friend and colleague, was inspecting the school. I happened to meet the sheikh at the hotel where I was staying. We started a conversation regarding my background and I told him what I did. A week later I was holidaying in India when Jacquie phoned me and said they wanted me to come and work here. That's how it all started. And eventually they offered Jacquie a job too. And we could take our animals. It was very flattering. It presented me with a challenge, one that I am so glad I accepted.

The school is beautifully situated and is very well resourced. It is expanding rapidly, now welcoming Emirate children as well as its international pupils. It's easier teaching there. The children are more motivated and the groups are smaller. I have to pinch myself and count my blessings constantly. I have reached my ambition, to teach science and to lead a great school, where I am loved and respected. This must surely be the icing on a unique cake, the culmination of a long and sometimes difficult career in teaching.

I was born in Chennai (India) and emigrated to the UK after the death of my first child. I was brought up in a Christian school in an English-speaking environment except at home – to my grandparents I spoke in Tamil but to my uncles it was English. Now I enjoy the best of both worlds, in terms of culture, food and the opportunity to use Indian languages with many working at the school.

Following the death of my daughter, I went to Scotland, where my mother was settled. My father had died and she had married again – a Scotsman. I was a chemistry graduate and had already got my Postgraduate Certificate of Education, but I had my baptism of teaching in a comprehensive school in the deprived Easterhouse region of Glasgow. Once pupils realised that this five foot Indian in a sari would not accept small missiles hurled at her I began to enjoy my short time there. My son was born while I was there and I later worked in a very good Catholic school in Stirling.

After the birth of my son my husband and I separated. He did not want anything to do with bringing up a child, having lost the daughter. It was his fear of losing another child. Then my stepfather died and my mother packed up everything to go back to India. So we all went. But, in spite of my qualifications and experience,

I could not get a proper job because I was divorced and single. The Christian community was not very happy with all that – at that time. Now it is all different.

It was a great sadness that I could not get the kind of job I wanted in India. Before I went to India, however, I had already been interviewed in London where the schools were desperate for maths and science teachers. They sent a telegram to me asking when I was coming back. I thought, 'At least somebody wants me.' I left my son with my mother. It was a difficult decision. He was only a year and a bit. I saw him again two years later on a holiday with friends from the UK. When he was five years old I brought him back with me to England. We managed, but it was tough. On arrival in London I was given a supply teacher's timetable with the instructions that Indians were only employed for supply. I declined this task very firmly and successfully fought for my rights. This taught me about discrimination against ethnic minorities and from then on I dedicated myself to serve this community.

The science fraternity and key long-time friends have since given me considerable support. A great head teacher from Bradford gave me the post of head of science in 1973 against the advice of the LEA and other professionals. Under her patronage I was able to experiment and develop a range of mid-management and senior-management skills. The team of teachers challenged and motivated many generations of girls from many cultures to be successful mothers with rewarding careers. With the help of colleagues I rose to be the head teacher.

I then wanted the challenge of managing a mixed school and I moved to one in Southall in January 1989. This school was called the 'Jewel in Ealing's Crown' as it had a very high academic standard with a flourishing sixth form – many going on to the best universities. Sadly, in 1993, the school had to close the sixth form due to reorganisation. I had fought desperately to retain the sixth form, threatening to leave if it went, but I lost against a strong

politically motivated opposition. I resigned and took early retirement. I could not face that school without a sixth form.

To be obliged to abandon the career and the role that I loved
was a bitter personal blow. I had to think seriously about a positive
future. After a short interval I became an Ofsted inspector. Then I
had an excellent opportunity to act as a science tutor for the Distance Learning PGCE for the independent sector. I was able to
visit and work with science departments in a range of independent
schools. This opened up a new experience – the education opportunities for the privileged few – which has been a great help to me
now that I work in an independent school. In 1997 I was accepted
as an inspector of teacher training.

Now I come back during the holidays or half term to do my
Ofsted work. It's a nice excuse to see how the house in London is
going and to monitor the development of science education. That
is the big pay-off for me. I see myself staying in the Emirates for as
long as they need me. Even when I stop doing things I may stay
there for half the year.

So it was that all the pieces of my life fell into place after my sixtieth year!

For me this teacher's journey started during the Second World War, when my mother's youngest brother taught a little six-year-old three major lessons – a love of reading, a love of animals and mastery of basic mathematical skills. He believed in me and gave me my first taste of successful teaching. At the age of fourteen my classmates in the girls' school bought me a small blackboard to teach them mathematics. A charismatic mathematics teacher at my high school helped me to star rank in the state school learning examinations. I knew then my life would be spent in education.

Generations of pupils, colleagues and close friends and family have all contributed to my great experiences. In 1991 I won the English Speaking Union scholarship for head teachers to visit the USA. I spent six weeks visiting schools and education authorities across the USA. My brief was to study strategies to raise the attainment of ethnic minorities and to write a report. The generosity and warmth of the educationists overwhelmed me. I learned what it was that made great teachers and charismatic visionary principals. At the centre of all their initiatives is a profound belief in the intrinsic worth of the individual and the value of a good education.

All this has undoubtedly prepared me for my major transitions, first in 1993 and then again in 2000. I was fifty-eight when I resigned from the school in Ealing. For the next seven years I did a lot of professional training. Which was a complete change. And fun. I am now doing what I enjoy most: teaching, leading a successful team and remaining involved in the front line of teacher training. Parents at this school deeply value the contribution the team is making to shaping the current and future generations. Every day, here, I know we are contributing to a change that is worthwhile. Life has never been better.

SUKEY FIELD

Chasing serenity

To be gay was not easy for a woman in the recent past. Sukey Field describes how her life has changed in her sixties.

For some time now in my life I have been pursuing serenity rather than radical transformation; attempting to get better at doing less, rather than finding new things to do or new ways to be. I want this decade to be one of change and reinvention but not one to be measured by how much I've got done or what radical change I have achieved. I have always been glad to be gay. Now, well into my sixties, I confess that it scarcely impinges on my everyday life. I have never lost my sense of identity as a gay woman but, as in other ways, I have mellowed out of it all. When my last relationship ended ten years ago I thought, 'That's it, I don't want to be doing this any more.' So much of my energy had gone into keeping my partner happy, because my happiness depended on hers. It would, I felt, be more rewarding if I spent that energy and

199

time on my friends. Sex bothers me not at all. I seem to get all the pleasures of the senses I need from good food and wine and sunny days, from exercise, nice places, music and, most important, from those good friendships.

I am convinced that I have been a lesbian all my life. Having said that, I have to admit that I was blissfully unaware of this until

about the age of twelve, when I developed my first major crush, and – like the leopard – knew I couldn't change my spots.

It was not for want of trying. Growing up gay in the Sixties and even Seventies was not particularly easy. It was fine to waft around with flowers in your hair, stoned to the eyeballs, sleeping around with Tom, Dick and Harry. It was much less fine to want to sleep around with other girls. Having tried to conform with a miserable variety of dorks and anoraks, I finally did find a really nice guy. We

got married. It was a disastrous choice on my part – I had everything a nice girl could want, but it just didn't work. Hard to explain, but I absolutely understand those men who know they are really women or vice versa – you just feel you're in the wrong skin.

Leaving my marriage was an enormous relief but brought with it all the attendant trials of coming out to friends, family and at work. Family was more difficult than the others I suppose, but I was luckier than some and it really wasn't that bad. In some ways it was made easier by my mother's persistent confusion about lesbianism and vegetarianism. By some quirk of fate I had decided to be a vegetarian at more or less the same time as I 'became' a lesbian, and my mother could never distinguish between the two. 'I never realised that all those tennis stars were vegetarian too,' she would announce; or very confidentially to someone offering me a plate of smoked salmon, 'No, my daughter's a lesbian you know – she doesn't eat fish.' This became so funny that it went some way to removing the sting of her disapproval and dislike of the turn I had taken.

Working in an organisation and being 'out' was, however, fraught with often indirect disapproval or plain unpleasantness. For a while you can rationalise that it just goes with the territory but it can get you down. Back in the Seventies and Eighties men still mostly assumed that lesbians were really frustrated chaps or weren't pretty enough to hook a real man. Straight women gave you a wide berth and/or thought you gave feminists a bad name. Management walked round the subject like hot coals, particularly if their staff had any involvement or responsibility for working with young(er) people – as I did. I don't think this issue blighted my career – there were far too many other ways in which I didn't do well in organisations – but I certainly realised that I could do without their implicit disapproval and their lack of acceptance of gay people. One incident in particular sticks with me, when the Director summoned me about plans for me to take on a short-term assignment abroad. The conversation went like this:

> HIM: We are quite prepared for you to go as long as you go alone and stay alone. You will need to be very mobile and ready to go off on visits at the drop of a hat etc.
> ME: O . . . well my sister is living in a neighbouring country and we had planned for her to come and visit me.
> HIM: That's fine of course, no problem.
> ME: So what are you saying?
> HIM: Well, umm (*shifting in his chair*) we don't want you to go with a partner or er . . . we really don't want to

upset anyone blah blah . . . (*and then the old cliché*) Don't get me wrong some of my best friends are homosexuals.

That conversation still rankles! But I also know that particular organisation would not behave like that now. Things do change.

But on the whole I think I have been lucky with work. I have mostly been involved with jobs where the end justified the means rather than the other way round. I was doing things I enjoyed and believed in. Finally, however, going freelance was the only escape from organisations, places that I found less and less tolerable. It was not the work itself, which I enjoyed. It was some of my colleagues and, particularly, the people who ran things who got me down. I know very few organisations where ideologies and ethics prevail over 'pragmatism' and profit. And if your ideologies and ethics are of a feminist or 'gender' persuasion, forget it. You can spin out the time but you will find yourself bumping into glass walls as well as the proverbial ceiling.

Most of my career has been involved with working in aid and development. The last two decades I have focused on gender equity issues within that context, attempting to plan projects and programmes in developing countries which enhanced women's positions in their communities or which at the very least did not continue to disadvantage them.

I have been an independent 'consultant' (a catch-all word for anyone working independently of an organisation) for the last fifteen years. Although I have been based in the UK all this time the work has also involved working visits to countries in the Pacific, Far East, East and Southern Africa, but most particularly in South Asia – where I was born and brought up until the age of ten. I am a third generation 'colonial' so I suppose there was an inevitability about wanting to work in those countries rather than just in the UK and Europe.

Now, though, I've had enough of travelling for work and only feel like travelling for holidays where I don't have to exert myself any more than slipping gently into the sea or gazing raptly at exotic animals while they gaze disapprovingly at me. It is all part of taking things easier.

One of the great and positive changes about being sixty is the pension and the release from the treadmill of earning an (entire) income. For two years I took time out from working for money and studied for an MA instead. The writing was hell but the learning and the reading was fun, interesting and richly rewarding. It gave me a new take on subjects I'd got tired of. At a time when my memory is getting very tricky and my physique increasingly pear-shaped it is good to engage with new issues and to feel that there is something that still excites the mind.

It is not all unalloyed pleasure, of course. I do feel physically less fit and more vulnerable. If I hurt myself I don't mend as quickly or as well as I did. I am painfully aware of all the appalling diseases that are lurking in the background waiting to strike one down. I definitely feel more anxious about myself than I did before. And there are things I know I'll never do again, like run a half-marathon, drink like a fish and not get a headache in the morning, or even stay up all night at parties. I know there are shining examples of super-oldies who do all these things but I'm not going to be one of them.

I think our generation has been more fortunate than that of our mothers, who did not have the assurances of staying healthier longer or the changing attitudes to singleness or 'old age'. Being single and/or doing things with other women is more acceptable and we can have more control of our lives to do what we want instead of what we ought. I certainly feel, as a woman on my own, that there is all the freedom I could want to make my own choices about how I wish to live and use my resources.

WENDY BALL

Granny's silver medal

What do you do for afters when you have spent the first part of your life building a family of six children of mixed races? If you are Wendy Ball you first become a conference organiser and then, come sixty, you go into professional garden design – and surprise yourself.

The main delight in recent years has lain in at last having more time to pursue my own interests, to travel with my husband or on my own, and in the arrival of five enchanting grand-children. The great challenge last year was to undertake a professional course in garden design. What fun it was to find that geometry learned fifty or so years before was actually relevant to technical drawing and that the brain, though taxed, hadn't totally atrophied. As the granny of the group, I was determined to keep up to the standard set by my younger colleagues. As graduates we designed a courtyard garden for Chelsea in 2001 and achieved a silver medal. This was something I never expected to do. But, then, nor did I expect to find myself with a mixed-race family of six children, four of them adopted, nor to be responsible for organising scientific conferences for 1500 scientists from all parts of the world. Life is full of surprises, I have found, with even more of them as I grow older.

I was born in Kettering in 1939, just before the outbreak of the Second World War. The future must have looked bleak to those around me, but I was lucky enough to be sent to live, with my mother, with my grandparents in Cambridge. The occasional trip to the air raid shelter in the middle of the night, armed with candles and cocoa, seemed a great adventure to a small child and the celebration of VE-Day was a joyous early memory.

My parents met as undergraduates at Cambridge, he a natural scientist and she a linguist. They subsequently went to Nigeria, where my father was a colonial officer, but my mother was unable to stand the heat, so they returned to England. My father started to run a boys' club in Corby, but served as a training pilot during the war and returned to the club afterwards. By 1946 three more children had been born. When I asked my mother why she had continued to produce so many children when life was so precarious, she astonished me by saying 'to help the war effort'!

I was a placid child, enjoying most subjects at school. Life proceeded reasonably smoothly, the only minor disruption being the removal of my family to Dorset when I was twelve. I did rather resent exchanging my excellent grammar school in Stamford for a very tinpot private school, where the girls were mostly preparing to 'come out'. A move to Shaftesbury High School improved matters, but the teaching was limited (science was virtually unknown). When I ventured that I was interested in pursuing architecture, the only response was that my maths were not good enough – I had been in the top set at Stamford, but had been taught very little since then. Sadly, it never occurred to me to question this, or do anything to remedy the situation, something I now regret, as I have become increasingly fascinated by town planning in later years.

However, reasonably well taught in French and German, I left to read for an external degree for London University, based in an Oxford finishing school, thinly disguised as a teaching establishment. While improving my German in Vienna before starting on my degree I met, and within three days became engaged to, my future husband, who was reading English at Oxford, so it seemed that the gods were smiling on us!

Armed with a degree but unable to decide on a career, we started our family, with the notion that I would be able to work later while still young. Helen and Diana were duly born, but by 1963 we thought the world too uncertain a place into which to bring more children (it was Bay of Pigs time and in London people were preparing to go down into their cellars with stacks of baked beans). As this was before the era of both the Pill and Abortion Law Reform, there were literally thousands of children in care throughout the country, a great many of whom were of mixed race and therefore considered virtually unadoptable, particularly the boys.

When we applied to adopt, we were met with disbelief and were told in no uncertain terms that it was out of the question as it would not be possible to match backgrounds! It took much patient persuasion to convince authorities that this was unnecessary, but eventually we were allowed to adopt David and were even given a layette as a reward. Yasmin, Peter and Richard all followed fairly rapidly, as, by now, the social workers were on their knees, begging us to take more. At the point where we had six children under ten we called a halt despite their pleas.

So the pattern of my life was really dictated by the goings on in Washington! The creation of a mixed-race family has for the last forty years been the main focus around which all my interests in the arts, music and creativity have had to be fitted. It has been fascinating to try to evaluate the nature/nurture debate, and to watch the children's individual and very different personalities emerge from five different genetic backgrounds. The children themselves

have been remarkable, coping well most of the time with the oddity of their family make-up, supported by wonderful friends and relations.

Over the years I completed a secretarial course, a City and Guilds course in Fashion and Design, organised concerts and other events for charity, and worked part-time for an architect, but in midlife it became important to earn some real money to buy a house. We had always lived in college houses, but needed to have the flexibility of house ownership. I reviewed my skills realistically and rigorously, then consulted a good friend who had always said there was a job for me in his department running conferences. He soon rang me to ask whether I would like to organise a major scientific conference his department was too busy to handle. I had three hours to make up my mind before the European organisation rang – if I said 'no', Oxford would lose the conference. So, like a fool, I found myself running a conference for 1500 scientists spread over nine colleges and umpteen lecture theatres! It was probably the steepest learning curve of my life. All human life was there, from the American woman throwing a tantrum because her medieval college room was not near a shower, to the little old man who said, 'Thank you so much, you have made me feel like a very small boy in a very large sweetshop.'

This career continued for some years, until we finally bought and converted a little Victorian shed in the middle of Oxford, which has been our delightful home since 1988. We were also able to build a new house right behind it, thus giving me a chance to exercise my latent architectural interests. Then came the professional garden design course and the surprise of the silver medal at the Chelsea Flower Show.

This, surely, is one of the bonuses of age – that there are still pleasant and even exciting surprises out there. There is more opportunity available than ever before and I can see no immediate prospect of retiring to a chaise longue with a good book. I am embarking on watercolour painting, another long-felt desire, and am currently trying to combine making clothes with garden design, with improving my languages (I added Italian along the way), with as much grannying as possible, not to mention all the concerts, films, plays etc. I want to see. The days are never long enough and nor, with good health, will they ever be.

What have been the pitfalls, disasters, triumphs and joys? I have been immensely fortunate in being born in England, to loving parents, and enjoying good health, good food and education. Looking back, I wish I had given myself longer before marrying and raising children. Greater maturity would have benefited all of us. The discovery that one of our sons was mildly autistic was sad, but he more than fulfilled his potential before he died, much missed, at the age of thirty-one. Other problems have been comparatively small and always balanced by the good things – children becoming viable adults, gorgeous grandchildren and now enough money to be able to choose from a variety of directions for the next era. Gather ye rosebuds . . .

WINNIE SMIKLE

Filling the vacuum

It must be devastating to be told that you are surplus to requirements in your fifties while doing the job you love and have done all your life. Winnie Smikle describes how she filled the vacuum in her life.

Yes there really is life after paid work and life for me began not at forty but at the age of fifty-two. I have been fortunate to follow the career I dreamt of since childhood. Now, however, I am involved with some things I always wanted to do, but was unable to while in paid employment. Life has taken on a new meaning and I can honestly say that I am enjoying everything I do.

After many years working as a nursing sister I had become a neighbourhood nurse manager in the Wandsworth Health Authority. Then there was yet another period of restructuring – and there had been many during my years of nursing. At the age of fifty-two I was surplus to requirement and was told I could work part-time if I wanted to. Eventually, after a stressful and unsettled period, I was retired on grounds of organisational change.

At the time I felt that my world had crumbled. I am fortunate to have a very supportive husband and many loyal friends who helped and supported me through what was a difficult period. I needed to fill the vacuum in my life – from leading a hectic and full life I now had time on my hands.

To fill this vacuum I went to college and did courses in Sociology, Counselling Skills and Massage (Physical Therapy). I began to do voluntary work for the Shaftsbury Society, became visiting co-ordinator for my church and was on the committee for a local Abbeyfield home. I felt that I needed a reason to get out of bed in the mornings, so every day was filled with some activity.

I am now involved in the following:

1   Managing a small residential home for three residents – which I refer to as my 'matchbox'. In this case, small is beautiful as the staff and I aim to provide a home-from-home environment. We are able to meet the needs of these three people – and to provide individualised care.
2   My husband and I are registered foster carers for the borough in which we live. We foster teenage young people and have found this to be challenging and rewarding. We aim to provide stability and some routine to the lives of these young people in our home.
3   Church involvement. I was brought up in a Christian home and have been a Christian for many years. I enjoy being part of a lively and warm church family. At present I am deputy churchwarden, a member of the parochial church council and involved with prayer ministry. I was also on the selection panel for our present vicar.
4   With the help of another retired nurse, we run a screening clinic at an Age Activity Centre. In line with the government

health targets, we check blood pressures, test urine, check weights and give advice when we can. Patients are referred to GPs when the need arises. This is a lively club for people aged over fifty-five. It provides companionship, nourishing meals, and activities such as bridge, dominoes, keep fit classes, indoor gardening and a lively choir every Wednesday afternoon.

5 I am a member of the League of Friends of Springfield Hospital and on the board of trustees. We meet about ten times yearly to allocate funds and to discuss investment from properties owned by the League. Money is allocated to the wards and community homes to improve the quality of life for patients suffering from mental illness.

6 I am mental health manager for a nursing home in Sandhurst, Berkshire. My special remit is to attend managers' hearings and to be an independent advocate for patients who are detained under sections of the Mental Health Act.

213

7   I am general secretary for the Friends of the Heart Founda-
     tion of Jamaica Ltd. With the help of the council and
     members of the organisation we hold several fund-raising
     events annually in order to buy medical supplies to send to
     the Heart Foundation of Jamaica. This is hard work, which
     takes time, effort and commitment.

8   I am also a gardener at heart – not that good at it – but I enjoy
     pottering in our small back garden. I grow vegetables and
     herbs. It gives me enjoyment, satisfaction, inner strength and
     tranquillity to tend the plants, watch them grow and share
     runner beans, tomatoes, peppers, thyme and corn with
     family and friends. I enjoy cooking – primarily West Indian
     meals for my family, having dinner parties, baking, reading,
     going to the theatre, visiting garden centres and museums,
     pottering about in my garden and being a grandmother.

While I was so busy doing all these things my husband was
getting exasperated about the many activities I was involved with.
He started to say that he had to make appointments to be able to
see me so he decided that he would go to Jamaica for a while. He
was away for four months and during that time I realised just what
I was doing to our many years of marriage. In a way, I felt the need
to fill my life to be able to cope with the sudden change but was
blinkered to what else was happening. This was thinking time for
me. I have subsequently curtailed some of my activities – but still
lead a very busy existence and try to involve him in some of the
things I do.

It is all a long way from my early years in Jamaica.

During the 1950s it was not always easy to train as a nurse in
Jamaica. Training places were limited to a few hospitals. The professions that most women pursued were nursing, teaching or secretarial work. My lifelong ambition was to be a nurse, so one of my
teachers advised my father to encourage me to apply to a hospital

in England for training, while I was waiting for a place in Jamaica. I applied and was accepted at St Crispin's Hospital in Duston, Northampton when I was nineteen years old. This was quite a step for a country girl. I had never left home for any period before, except for the odd holiday in Kingston with an aunt.

I arrived in England, thousands of miles from home, leaving behind my family, friends and familiar surroundings. To make the change even more traumatic, it was in the middle of winter. I never thought that I could survive the initial climatic change, but here I am, many years later and so settled that I feel very much at home.

I qualified as a registered mental nurse, registered general nurse, registered midwife and registered district nurse. As students we were the main workforce and the hours on duty were long. It was the norm to do a forty-eight-hour week. At the end of my initial training I got married and had two children. It was quite a juggling act, coping with them, running a home and doing a demanding job. My husband has always been very supportive – so, between us, we managed.

Hindsight is a wonderful thing. Looking back, I realise just how fortunate I am to have the opportunity to be so involved at this stage of my life. When I was forced to give up paid work, that period was for me the start of a more fulfilling and rewarding life. I always wanted to run my own little nursing home. My 'postage stamp' is very satisfying. I am privileged that, at the age of sixty-three, I am able to give something back to the society in which I live and from which I have gained so much.